Getting Started with Transmedia Storytelling

a practical guide for beginners
2nd edition

by Robert Pratten

ISBN: 1515339165

ISBN-13: 978-1515339168

For Helen.

Without whom none of this would be possible.

CONTENTS

INDEX OF FIGURES

1 INTRODUCTION

This document is a kind of choose your own adventure. Although it follows a notional workflow from project inception through to completion, many of the ideas are complementary so feel free to dive into those sections that interest you most and span out from there. For those that prefer a more structured approach I'd suggest starting here and reading through to the end of the book.

The unique selling point of this book is that it focuses on the practicalities of writing multi-platform stories that invite audience participation. The dotted shape in Figure 1, labeled *Active Story System*, illustrates the relative attention given by this book to each of four important areas required to deliver a working solution: experience, story, project management & organization[1]

Figure 1 The focus of this book

1.1 FIRST SOME DEFINTIONS

Before going much further I think it's worthwhile to definite some common terms that I'll be using throughout the book.

Channel	this is a method of communication such as video, audio, image, live event, text and so on
Media	this refers to the embodiment of the channel such as a text file, an mp4 file, an mp3 file, a jpg file, a poster, a banner ad

---

[1] Organization = the people or company required to deliver the story-experience.

Platform   this is something that supports the channel & media such as YouTube, Soundcloud, Flickr, a shopping mall, a cinema, a web site and so on

Format   this is a common arrangement of platforms and channels or experience characteristics and participation mechanics

Device   something that allows the audience to access the platforms such as a PC, a tablet computer, a mobile phone and so on.

"Experience characteristics" and "participation mechanics" are not commonly used terms but ones I invented when working on the Transmedia Playbook[2]. They refer to common building blocks or aspects that make certain experiences similar enough to group them into a type – like the Alternate Reality Game (ARG), for example. But more on this later!

1.2 WHAT IS TRANSMEDIA?

I'd like to present several definitions of transmedia storytelling – first the more widely recognized definition and then some alternatives.

A traditional definition of transmedia storytelling would be:

> telling a story across multiple platforms, preferably allowing audience participation, such that each successive platform heightens the audience' enjoyment.

To do this successfully, the embodiment of the story in each media needs to be satisfying in its own right while enjoyment from all the media should be greater than the sum of the parts – as illustrated in Figure 2.

The problem with the traditional definition is that it is focuses on the *how* of transmedia storytelling and not the *why* – it describes the production and not the consumption. If instead we place the audience at the center of the definition then we get much better focus for our work. Now transmedia storytelling could be described as:

> taking the audience on an emotional journey that goes from moment-to-moment.

A "moment" is a point in time when we are totally absorbed in the present. Most of our lives are spent in an endless stream of events that mean little or nothing to us; time is like running water – we don't notice the millions of tiny droplets that make up the stream. We want to take one or more of these millions of tiny droplets of time and make them mean something more – we want to make them memorable and meaningful… to make them a moment.

With this second definition we can say that **transmedia storytelling is a design philosophy**. It's a design

---

2   http://www.slideshare.net/tstoryteller/playbook-online-v10

philosophy that is still in in infancy even though many people have been telling multi-platform stories for a long time. The crucial difference between transmedia storytelling and multiplatform storytelling is the attempt to create synergy between the content and a focus on an emotional, participatory experience for the audience. Simply throwing up a website for your TV show doesn't make transmedia storytelling – especially if there's no story – even if it might commonly be refer to as such.

Figure 2 What is Transmedia?

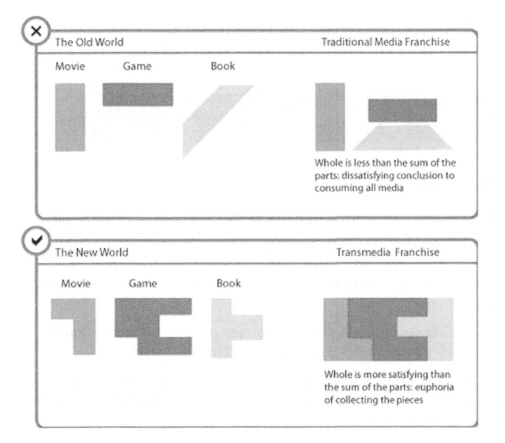

Let's ask ourselves two questions:

- Why tell stories?

- Why tell stories across multiple platforms?

1.2.1 WHY TELL STORIES?

We tell stories to entertain, to persuade and to explain.

Our minds do not like random facts or random objects and so they create their own stories to make sense of otherwise discrete, isolated events and items. We naturally and often subconsciously connect the dots.

And dots connected in a stimulating way we call great stories.

Great stories win hearts and minds.

As an example of the power of stories, check out Significant Objects[3]. The project team bought thrift store junk on eBay for $128.74 (never spending more than $1 or $2 per item) and then re-listed it with an added story… to make the object significant. The results was a whopping revenue of $3,612.51

Figure 3 The power of story: Results from Significant Objects

1.2.2 WHY MULTIPLE PLATFORMS?

We tell stories across multiple platforms because no single media satisfies our curiosity and no single platform our lifestyle.

We are surrounded by an unprecedented ocean of content, products and leisure opportunities. The people to whom we wish to tell our stories have the technology to navigate the ocean and can choose to sail on by or stop and listen.

Technology and free markets have allowed unprecedented levels of customization, personalization and responsiveness such that a policy of "one size fits all" is no longer expected or acceptable.

Telling stories across multiple platforms allows content that's right-sized, right-timed and right-placed to form a larger, more profitable, cohesive and rewarding experience. Only with transmedia storytelling can we place the audience at the center of what we do.

---

[3] http://significantobjects.com/

Figure 4 Place the audience at the center of any experience design

1.2.3   THE PROMISE AND DEMANDS OF 21ST CENTURY STORYTELLING

Figure 5 shows the opportunity of transmedia storytelling to fuse together benefits and fun for the consumer with promotion and feedback to the producer. Good transmedia storytelling should have a duality of purpose and only reveal itself as one thing or another when measured in a particular way – much like the electron that has wave-particle duality[4].

It's vitally important for the commercial success of a project that the marketing communications and customer feedback mechanisms are built into the storytelling and experience design because the audience avoids and mistrusts advertising. By adopting this entertainment-marketing duality, the audience will advocate on your behalf and share content because it meets their personal and social needs, not because you have bribed them with promised rewards.

To accomplish this, we must write experiences that combine personalization, participation, cross-platform communication and social connecting as shown in Figure 6. This book explains how to accomplish this.

---

[4] http://en.wikipedia.org/wiki/Wave%E2%80%93particle_duality

Figure 5 Blending entertainment and marketing

Figure 6 How we need to write our stories

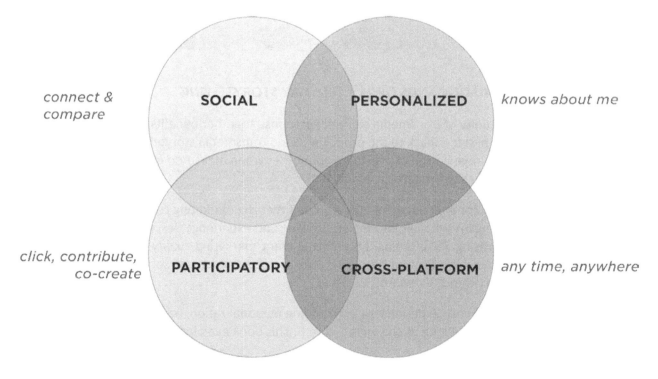

1.2.4 HENRY JENKINS: 7 PRINCIPLES

Henry Jenkins is the Provost's Professor of Communication, Journalism, and Cinematic Arts at the University of Southern California. To put his transmedia thinking into context, the origin of his work is from the study of fans, fandom and popular culture. He is interested in how fans are rewarded by transmedia storytelling and what aspects of a transmedia storyworld create engagement and community.

A full description of Henry Jenkins' 7 principles can be found on his blog[5].

Note that below where you read "vs" the two dimensions are not in opposition but describe two axes on a table - such as the spreadable vs drillable in Figure 7.

My interpretation of Henry's principles characterize transmedia properties as follows:

Spreadability vs Drillability	Spreadability refers to the motivation and ease with which content can be circulated by fans through social media.

Drillability is the extent to which fans explore the storyworld by "digging deeper" to discover hidden gems. Note that when Henry quotes Jason Mittell (from whom the term drillability originates) he uses the phrases "forensic fandom" and "magnets for engagement".

Figure 7 Spreadability vs Drillability

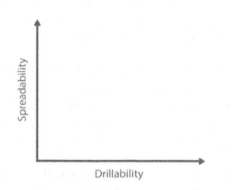

Continuity vs Multiplicity	Continuity refers to the consistency of the storyworld across the many embodiments of it. That is, as a fan discovers (drills down) more content does it all make sense? Meaning that there are no contradictions nor inconsistencies.

Multiplicity refers to "alternative retellings" or parallel universes in which the same stories get retold in a different setting. The reward for fans is a fresh perspective on the familiar but, as Henry warns, creators need to

---

[5] http://henryjenkins.org/2009/12/the_revenge_of_the_origami_uni.html

clearly communicate that this is a retelling and stay consistent to the storyline.

Figure 8 Continuity vs Multiplicity

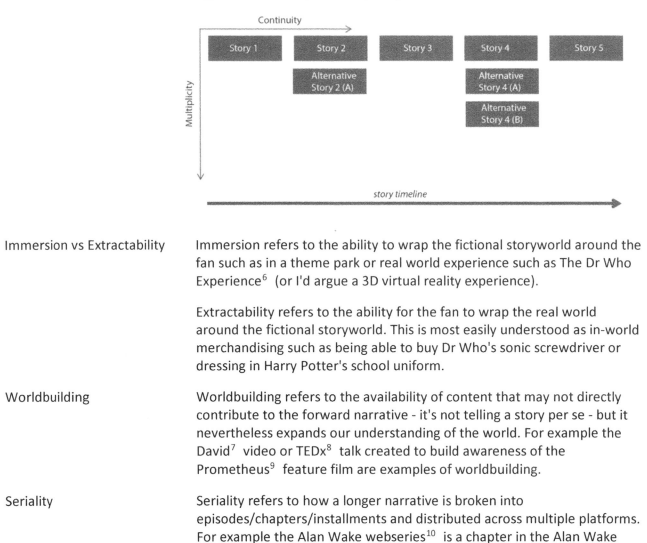

| | | | | |
| Immersion vs Extractability | Immersion refers to the ability to wrap the fictional storyworld around the fan such as in a theme park or real world experience such as The Dr Who Experience[6] (or I'd argue a 3D virtual reality experience). |

Extractability refers to the ability for the fan to wrap the real world around the fictional storyworld. This is most easily understood as in-world merchandising such as being able to buy Dr Who's sonic screwdriver or dressing in Harry Potter's school uniform.

Worldbuilding — Worldbuilding refers to the availability of content that may not directly contribute to the forward narrative - it's not telling a story per se - but it nevertheless expands our understanding of the world. For example the David[7] video or TEDx[8] talk created to build awareness of the Prometheus[9] feature film are examples of worldbuilding.

Seriality — Seriality refers to how a longer narrative is broken into episodes/chapters/installments and distributed across multiple platforms. For example the Alan Wake webseries[10] is a chapter in the Alan Wake story - it tells the prequel to the story in the Alan Wake Xbox game.

---

[6] http://www.doctorwhoexperience.com/
[7] http://www.youtube.com/watch?v=1Es_JimQFXw
[8] http://www.youtube.com/watch?v=jb7gspHxZiI
[9] http://www.imdb.com/title/tt1446714/
[10] http://www.youtube.com/show/alanwakebrightfalls

Subjectivity	Subjectivity refers to the range of points of view from different characters. Typically this is thought of in terms of secondary or supporting characters that get to express their point of view on a different platform to where the hero is telling his story.
Performance	Performance refers to the ability or extent to which fans contribute to the storyworld - perhaps by creating fan fiction or mashups of a videos or role-playing in the storyworld.

1.2.5   JEFF GOMEZ: 10 COMMANDMENTS

Jeff Gomez is CEO of Starlight Runner Entertainment. I received his ten commandments at a packed presentation to the StoryWorld conference in Los Angeles in the summer of 2012 in his talk "The 10 Commandments of 21st Century Franchise Production". What I present below is my interpretation of Jeff's instructions which may differ from his exact intention or even from what he actually said! Regardless of the degree of accuracy, his laws of transmedia franchise development – or my interpretation of them – are worth following:

Know the brand essence	Understand what's at the heart (the essence) of the storyworld that delivers so much pleasure to the audience. Core to this is what I refer to as the premise (the "truth" the author wishes to convey) but it's more than that, it's also the tone and themes.
Storyworld rules all	All production stakeholders from creative to marketing to legal must put aside their personal preferences, ambitions and rivalries in order to best serve the franchise
Put up tent poles	Everyone on the production team must know where the storyworld is heading. Hence the visionaries that guide the storyworld must provide adequate forward stepping stones and direction – even if that direction is changed at a later date.
Hire the best...	...but don't let the superstars roadblock the ongoing development.
Organize resources	for canon and assests. That is, a. provide a comprehensive living document such as a story bible or franchise bible that everyone on the team has access to and b. some form of centralized content management system that contains approved assets. This ensures consistency across all stakeholders.
Establish a clearing house	A steering group of representatives from the major stakeholders must meet regularly to guide the franchise and storyworld forward – recommending, sharing, discussing new initiatives and heading off potential conflicts of interest.

Incentivize stakeholders to support the franchise strategy beyond the initial roll out.

Validate audience participation and celebrate it! Provide a process and opportunities for fans and stakeholders to enter into a dialogue about what's coming up and exchange opinions.

Licensing, marketing and merchandise **must expand the narrative of the storyworld** such that everything available for fans to collect is worthwhile owning.

Be accessible and additive across a range of "portals" (e.g. entry points) so that regardless of how fans enter the storyworld the experience is always satisfying.

1.2.6   ROBERT PRATTEN: 7 TENETS OF FUTURE STORYWORLDS

We can see that Henry and Jeff's principles and commandments are complimentary and address different aspects – Jeff's of course much more the commercial issues of making Henry's principles happen.

I come at transmedia storytelling from yet another angle. Both Henry and Jeff are predominately referring to large franchises whereas my interests are in creating a living, breathing alternative reality in which anyone can choose to pretend that the fictional world of their choice does actually exist.

Figure 9 represents the seven design goals I set myself for creating persistent, immersive worlds that blend reality and fiction.

Figure 9 Seven Tenets of Future Storyworlds

PERVASIVE	PERSISTENT	PARTICIPATORY	PERSONALIZED	CONNECTED	INCLUSIVE	CLOUD-BASED
Available on any device, anywhere and at any time. Blurs real world and fictional world.	Story evolves even if you're not engaging with it. Aggregate audience activity and real-world environmental factors shape story development in real time.	Allows audience to interact with story characters, locations, things and each other.	Audience members have personalized experience based on past activity and permissions granted to storyworld.	The audience journey across touchpoints is intelligently managed to create a seamless, integrated experience.	The experience accommodates a range of devices and audience engagement styles such that it's not only users of expensive smart phones and tablets that get all the fun.	Network intelligence communicates with peripheral devices to deliver the other six tenets.

I believe that future storyworlds will have the following characteristics:

Pervasive   the story will be built around the audience – connecting with them across devices

Persistent   the story evolves over time, reacting to audience engagement

Participatory the audience interacts with characters and other audience members

Personalized the story remembers decisions and conversations and becomes tailored to each audience member

Connected   the experience connects across platforms and to the real world – allowing the story to be contextual such as integrating current weather conditions, tides, air quality and such like

Inclusive   a range of devices and engagement modes are accommodated so that as many people as possible are allowed to enjoy the story even if at different levels of depth and sophistication

Cloud-based a network intelligence controls the story and the experience from a central core – able to see all content and all the audience.

1.3   SUMMARY

To summarize then what transmedia storytelling is, it's an approach to audience engagement that seeks to integrate the three Cs (see Figure 10):

- Characters – the importance of story
- Convenience – the importance of getting the right content to the right people at the right time
- Community – the importance of connecting fans and rewarding them.

At the intersections we see the actions and functions we must support:

- Characters+Convenience – the personalization of the story experience for each person based on their relationship to the world

- Convenience+Community – the continued "personalization" but in a broader sense as applied to audience segments. For example an audience team collaborates to unlock content that only they can see. Also at this intersection is the ability to share content and refer friends to the world

- Community+Characters – this is the relationship between the community and the world. Creators should provide opportunities to strengthen the relationship through procedures and technology to allow fan contributions, character interactions and such like.

Figure 10 The three Cs of transmedia storytelling

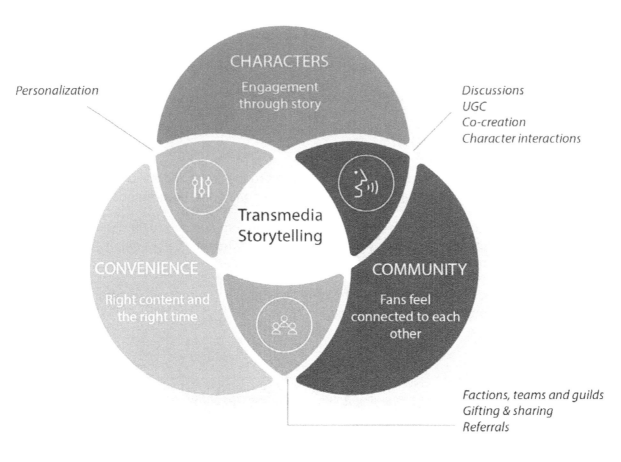

Personalization

CHARACTERS
Engagement
through story

Discussions
UGC
Co-creation
Character interactions

Transmedia
Storytelling

CONVENIENCE
Right content and
the right time

COMMUNITY
Fans feel
connected to each
other

Factions, teams and guilds
Gifting & sharing
Referrals

2   UNDERSTANDING TRANSMEDIA STORYTELLING

Transmedia storytelling is an umbrella term that encompasses many types of project from pervasive games and alternate reality games (ARG) to interactive web series and movie-book franchises. In truth there are few accepted and recognizable "formats" – only common tropes familiar to certain audiences.

What makes transmedia exciting and challenging is the combination of story and experience and how these can be combined in a multitude of ways. Nevertheless, I think it's useful to try to classify different types of story-experience into what might be thought of as a transmedia format.

2.1   WHAT TYPE OF STORY-EXPERIENCE ("FORMAT") IS RIGHT FOR YOU?

When scriptwriters write a screenplay, how many consider the audience's experience of the movie beyond the emotional engagement with the story? By which I mean, do they think of an audience sat in a cinema; or a couple kissing in the back row of a cinema; or someone with a TV-dinner watching at home? The same might be asked of novel writers – do they imagine their readers with book in hand on the beach or sat on an airplane?

I believe the best of all creative people will imagine their audience experiencing their art. That's what enables them to really optimize their creative – the story is in sync or in context with certain audience behavior.

Often the audience experience might be forgotten by some creatives because it's implied or assumed because of the medium: it's a film, it's a book etc. We know what these mediums are.

But a transmedia project can take many forms and guises. Additionally, we want to optimize the advantages that transmedia gives us which is to deliver the right content to the right device and at the right time. This means it's vital we understand the experience we're trying to create: not only the emotional engagement in the story but also in the engagement of the experience.

Commercial and practical considerations also play their part of course and may dictate the production of things that are easy/possible to sell which in turn must be incorporated into the story-experience.

To get started, thing here are five simple questions to help define or identify your story-experience:

1. What is the story I want to tell?
2. How will I deliver the story?
3. What kind of audience participation do I want or need?
4. How will audience participation affect the story over time?
5. How much is based in the real world vs a fictional world?

If you are taking a goal-orientated approach then you might find yourself starting with bullet point 3 and working around to find a story that supports the participation.

Figure 11 Getting Started: Five Questions

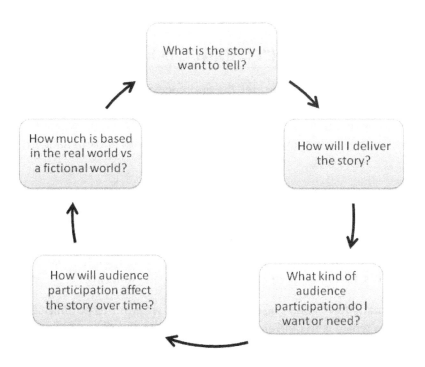

When thinking about delivering the story, put aside for now the specifics of particular platforms and think about the experience in terms of:

- the narrative spaces you want to cover (location, characters, time)
- the number and relative timing of the platforms (sequential, parallel, simultaneous, non-linear)
- the extent and type of audience involvement (passive, active, interactive, collaborative).

There's a lot to consider here but let's tackle it as a two-stage process:

- Step 1: decide the narrative space, number of platforms and their timing
- Step 2: decide the extent of audience involvement.

Figure 12 shows a "typical" franchise-type transmedia project. It's a series of single-platform deliverables - a book, a movie, a game. In many ways the platforms are independent except that they often cover different narrative spaces: prequel, sequel, flashback which may dictate a release order or schedule. In any case there's no apparent inter-dependence between the platforms.

Figure 12 Transmedia Franchise

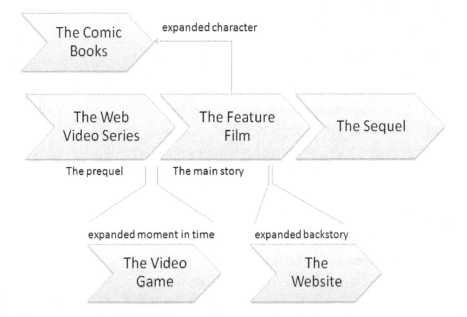

By contrast, an Alternate Reality Game (ARG), Figure 13, might cover a single narrative space across multiple platforms – each alone insufficient to carry the complete story but like jigsaw puzzle pieces they must be assembled to complete the picture (well… you know… story).

Figure 13 The Alternate Reality Game

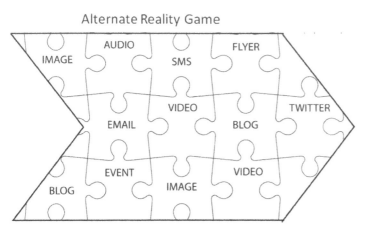

Multiple platforms contribute to single experience

These different types to transmedia can be represented by the diagram in Figure 14.   Of course it's also possible to combine different types of transmedia as shown in Figure 15.

Figure 14 Types of Transmedia

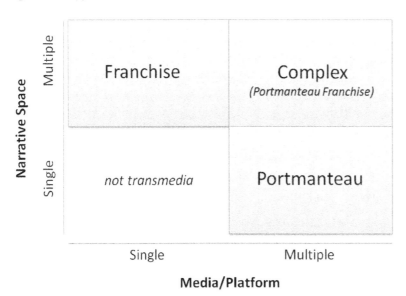

Figure 15 Mixing and Matching different types of transmedia

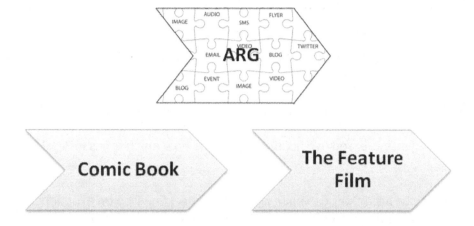

2.1.1 AUDIENCE INVOLVEMENT IN YOUR STORY

Audience involvement in the story often bothers creative people more familiar with non-interactive formats such as movies and books. It's not just that these people want to tell their story without interference; it's also the fear that amateur involvement will sully the final result. And for those who have tried involving audiences there's concerns about the effort of "community management" – the time and trouble to guide, motivate, appeal and appease.

It's not only creative people unfamiliar with non-interactive formats that worry about how to tell *their* story and yet still find room for audience participation. Talk to game designers about audience (i.e. player) interaction and story and they'll tell you that the more control you give to players (audiences), the less control is retained by the author.   In fact the problem is even more pronounced in MMOs where virtual world guru Richard Bartle[11] says "Virtual world designers can't add story, they can only add content. Content provides experiences that can be made by those who come through or observe them into story." So at its most open-ended, the virtual world (or transmedia experience) creates a world with lots of actionable content and choices but no plot?

This player-author struggle is tackled by games like Fallout 3 and Red Dead Redemption (both open-world AAA games) by offering players the choice to explore (create their own stories) or tackle quests (follow the author's story). Cut-scenes of course offer the most extreme authorial control and can be hated by some game players because they lose agency – that is, they lose the power to interact.

It's clear that transmedia experiences can borrow from the lessons of games and virtual worlds – creating a storyworld into which the author places a mix of story and content with opportunities for sit-forward and sit-back participation.

---

[11] http://www.amazon.com/Designing-Virtual-Worlds-Richard-Bartle/dp/0131018167

Looking further into audience participation I discovered the "storytelling cube" (Figure 16) first presented at the 2002 Game Developers Conference by Raph Koster and Rich Vogel to describe how narrative is explored in online virtual worlds. It applies particularly well to participatory experiences. The three axes are control, impact and context:

- Control: How much freedom does the audience have to create their own experience and how much control will you have as the author?

- Impact: What long-lasting impact will the audience have on the evolution of the experience?

- Context: How much of the experience is based in a fictional world and how much exists in "real life"?

There's no right or wrong position to be inside this cube: it's up to you to decide based on experience, preference and resources. At one extreme you might have an entirely fictional world, tightly controlled by the author with no audience interaction and at the other you could have an experience based around real-world places & events in which the audience is free to completely change how the story evolves and is experienced. And of course the two can be mixed and there's a lot of space in between.

Figure 16 Storytelling Cube (Raph Koster & Rich Vogel)

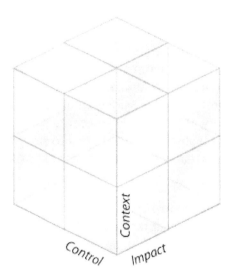

2.1.2 TRANSMEDIA RADAR DIAGRAM – SUMMARIZING YOUR FORMAT

When reading pitches and proposals at StoryLabs[12], I realized that what I really needed upfront from Producers was a very quick and easy way to see what type of experience I was about to discover. So, from this need to avoid lots of reading, I designed the Transmedia Radar Diagram as shown in Figure 17. Although there are some missing details that may help define your experience – such as use of time - it's a good start towards easily and quickly presenting your project.

The four axes on the radar diagram in Figure 17 represent:

- **importance of narrative** - how important is the story to the experience? What degree of authorial control is there?

- **importance of co-creation** - how important is it that the audience contribute to the story-experience? This is a spectrum of participation from clicking a link to creating content

- **importance of the real-world** - how important is it that the story-experience pervades real locations, places, events and people?

- **importance of gaming** - how important is it that the audience has a goal or must achieve or collect something?

There's no absolute scale for the four axes, it's their strength relative to each other. Of course, if you're comparing projects then they need to compare across projects too.

Figure 17 Transmedia Radar Diagram

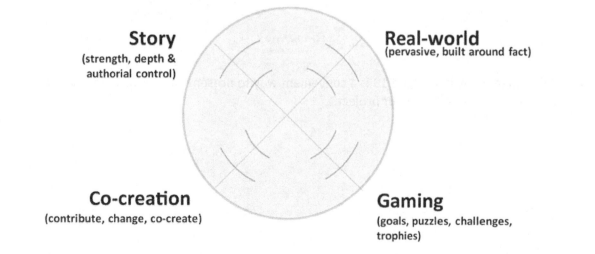

Story
(strength, depth & authorial control)

Real-world
(pervasive, built around fact)

Co-creation
(contribute, change, co-create)

Gaming
(goals, puzzles, challenges, trophies)

---

12 http://storylabs.us/

Figure 18 shows some common "formats" that readers might be familiar with to illustrate the use of the radar diagram.

Figure 18 Example formats as shown as radar diagrams

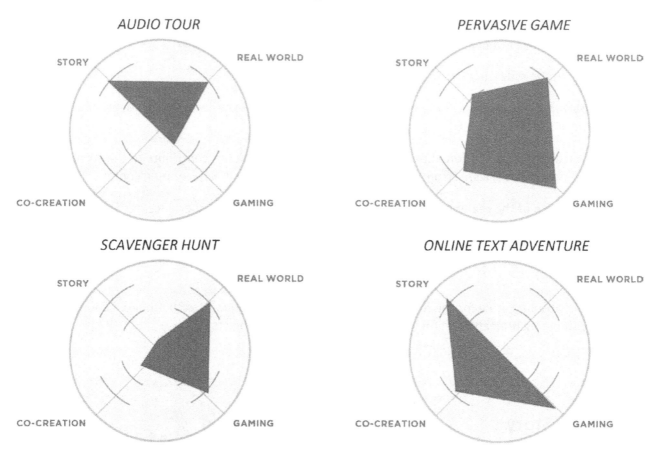

The one-page pitch sheet shown in Figure 19 is a convenient way to present your project and provides a framework for others to understand your project.

Figure 19 One-page Pitch Sheet

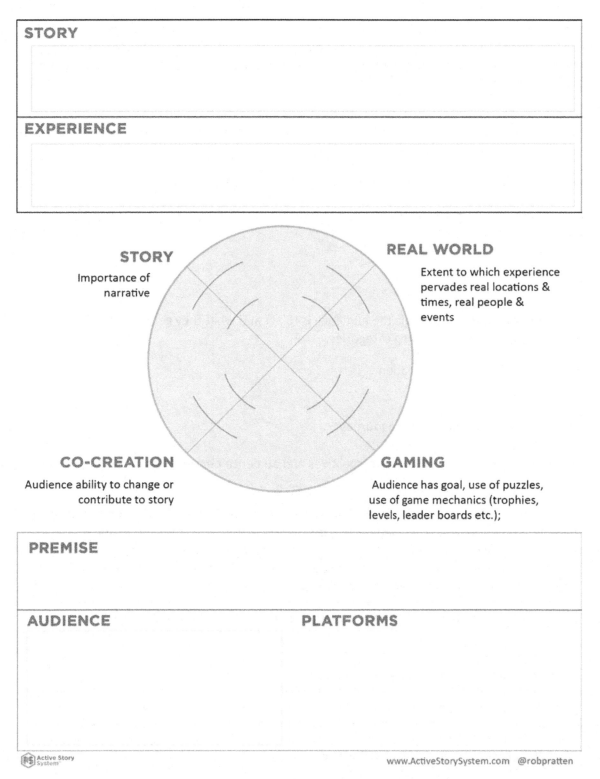

STORY

EXPERIENCE

STORY
Importance of narrative

REAL WORLD
Extent to which experience pervades real locations & times, real people & events

CO-CREATION
Audience ability to change or contribute to story

GAMING
Audience has goal, use of puzzles, use of game mechanics (trophies, levels, leader boards etc.);

PREMISE

AUDIENCE   **PLATFORMS**

Active Story System

2.2   SO ARE THERE TRANSMEDIA FORMATS?

I understand that creative people don't like to be tied down to definitions and rigid formats but when I'm dreaming up solutions and concepts I've found it very helpful to have a "lazy dog" or quick reference guide to provoke new ideas. That is, breaking down transmedia story-experiences into their component parts helps stimulate creativity, not stifle it.

In the Transmedia *Playbook*[13] that I worked on with the team for Conducttr[14], we defined "format" to mean a combination of *experience characteristics* and frequently used *participation mechanisms* (which in the playbook are called participation tropes).

Experience characteristics encompass how the audience experience is shaped by:

- Pacing (the use of time – usually schedule [as in date & time] vs on-demand [interactive])
- Solo or multiplayer options
- Personalization
- Story structure
- Use of the real world

Participation mechanics relate to how able the audience is to act and what they get in return. These mechanics were grouped into the following categories:

- Availability and control of information
- Use of counting and limits
- Use of exclusivity
- Flow or interruption of the audience journey
- Use of locations
- Use of perspectives – both character perspectives and audience perspectives
- Use of sharing.

For example, if you build a Twitter experience in which the audience has to make a decision by voting, the experience characteristics would be *scheduled pacing*, because you open and close the voting process at a certain period of time, *branching narrative story structure* because the outcome determines where the story goes next and *multiplayer play style* because the audience will work together and vote as a community. The participation mechanics are the *use of counting* (counting votes).

It's possible to argue that these two dimensions – experience characteristics and participation mechanics -

---

[13] http://www.slideshare.net/tstoryteller/playbook-online-v10

[14] A big thank you goes to Nataly Ríos Goicoechea, Belén Santa-Olalla and Eduardo Iglesias who work with me at Transmedia Storyteller Ltd and who put a lot of time into the Playbook. Also thanks to Ellie Mathieson who did the layout and illustrations. Apologies for the frequent references to Conducttr throughout but Alexey Ossikine and the technical team Oleg Lazutkin and Andrey Grunyov and I have been working on this technology since 2009 and it's formed a large part of my life in the periods between the books!

ought really to be one or maybe more than two but my goal was really just to attempt to formalize different types of transmedia experiences so that they can be better communicated to others and that as practitioners we have some basic structure for creating new experiences.

As you progress through the book we'll look in designing with these characteristics in mind.

2.3   KNOWING WHERE TO START

Knowing where to start can be the first challenge in creating a transmedia project. The problem is that the story and the *experience of the story* need to be in harmony.

As a producer, you might approach your project in this order:

- decide the **format** (e.g. the broad type of audience experience)
- develop the **storyworld** (e.g. the characters, locations, time periods and other attributes)
- develop **stories** that exist in the storyworld and play out across your format.

As a writer, you might approach your project in a different order:

- develop a **story**
- develop a **storyworld** that supports this story and many more (e.g. expand the characters, locations, time periods and other attributes)
- decide which **formats** could communicate the stories and the storyworld.

There's no right or wrong way and it usually depends on where the inspiration comes from or what opportunities you see. Also, because "transmedia" is such a broad umbrella, the start of the writing process can depend on the type of transmedia project you're creating. Figure 20 presents a flowchart for how to get started: if you plan a franchise-type project then you can just get started writing the first piece of media; if you plan a portmanteau-type project then you'll need to start by thinking through the experience.

In this book, I'm going to start with stories and storyworlds because it allows me to introduce some basic concepts.

2.3.1   WRITING FOR DIFFERENT PLATFORMS

While it's nice to think you might write a story independently of the platform, it's not entirely possible if you want to maximize the audience experience. You only have to take the example of great books that don't translate to movies - the problem is not the story but the failure to adapt it to the platform.

Section 6 is dedicated to writing for multiplatform, predominantly portmanteau-type interactive experiences but if you're thinking of a franchise-type transmedia project then I'd recommend that you start by writing for the platform you feel most comfortable with. Even if your high concept identifies stories on other platforms, complete most of one platform and then work on the others. You can then go back to modify or fix the first platform later but trying to write all platforms at the same time will create a monster headache that's worth avoiding!

Note too that it's going to be worth reading up on the specifics of writing for those other platforms because they all have their own rules and best practices.

There are many reference sources that will tell you what makes for a good story – none of which changes when you're writing for multiple platforms:

- You need a compelling hero character (protagonist) that people care about

- The character needs to overcome adversity: without adversity there is no conflict and without conflict there is no drama

- Character has a goal – something they must achieve

- Character has needs – typical a primary psychological need that usually fights against the goal (e.g. the need to be liked or the need to save face)

- Character evolves over the story – they start with hang-ups or ill-conceived views of the world and through tackling the adversity they emerge stronger and wiser

- three acts - a beginning (setup), middle (conflict) and end (resolution): setup the character and the goal quickly, throw lots of roadblocks at the character that challenge them and that provide learning opportunities (e.g. to deal with their issues) and then wrap up everything –usually hero achieves goal and better understands themselves or changes opinion.

Figure 20 How to get started with a franchise-type transmedia experience

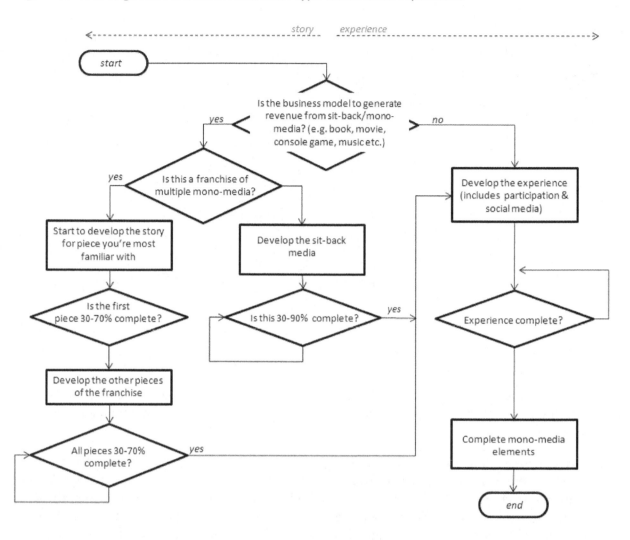

After the story is written for the first platform, you'll have source material that can be used to identify additional layers - either smaller exploration content[15] or wholly new complete works (see Figure 21).

---

[15] See Figure 98

Figure 21 Working from source material

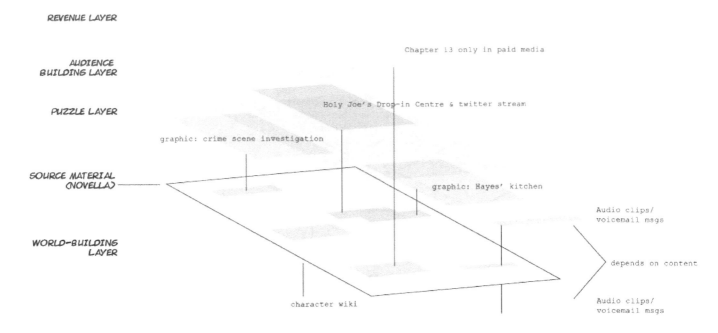

Figure 22 shows our approach with Lowlifes where we were keen that there should be limited overlap between platforms and that the principal character (the protagonist) of each platform remained the hero of their own media.

Figure 23 shows how we wanted a multiplying effect of multiplatform consumption! The idea here is that while Hayes' story is entertaining on its own, anyone who had read his wife's blog would get a double-kick from the ending because they had unique knowledge only blog readers would know. In fact, something similar to this happened to my wife and me while we were watching an episode of Project Runway[16]. In this particular episode, a member of the production team asked a designer to stop working on their costume and step outside where the cameras couldn't see them. For me this was a minor bit of drama but my wife gasped because she had insider knowledge having watched Models of the Runway[17] - the companion show that gave the model's perspective on events. She understood what was being said off camera because she'd pieced together the evidence from the other show. This is the kind of enhanced experience we want from transmedia – an emotional reward for engaging on more than one platform or channel.

---

[16] https://en.wikipedia.org/wiki/Project_Runway
[17] https://en.wikipedia.org/wiki/Models_of_the_Runway

Figure 22   "Missing chapters" across platforms

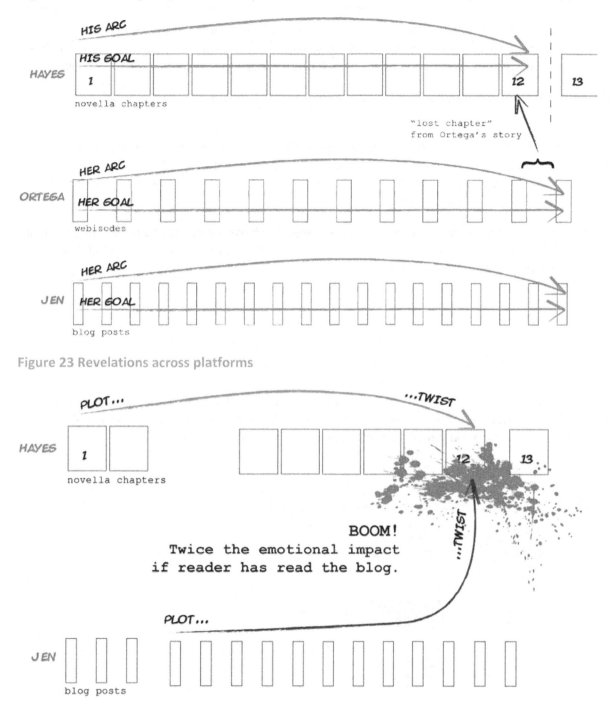

Figure 23 Revelations across platforms

2.4 STORY STRUCTURES

Instinctively or from experience we know what a story is: a hero, driven by a certain desire, battles to overcome adversity to achieve a goal. The craft of writing a good story is very hard to master and the best book I can recommend is John Truby's *The Anatomy of Story: 22 Steps to Becoming a Master Storyteller*[18].

I've read many scriptwriting books but John's book seems to be the most suited to transmedia storytelling.

What I'd like to introduce here is different story structures. Please remember that all stories have the same aim: to take the audience on a satisfying emotional journey. Typically this requires that we have empathy for the hero character and want them to succeed... but I'm going to assume that you know this and move on to discuss the delivery of story.

Figure 24 represents a linear story. The blocks could be pages of a book, chapters of a book, episodes in a TV series and so on. The important thing to note is that the audience only has one path through the story: start with episode one and end at episode three.

Figure 24 Linear story

In Figure 25 the audience has been given choices at the end of the episodes or chapters and is allowed to branch off in different directions. A "choose your own adventure" story is like this. This approach is called a branching narrative because the narrative branches at certain decision points.

Figure 25 Branching narrative

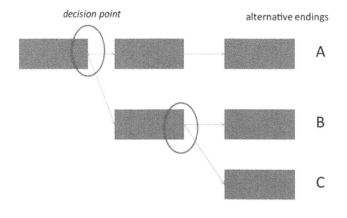

---

[18] http://www.amazon.com/The-Anatomy-Story-Becoming-Storyteller/dp/0865479933

Although this can work really well in the right circumstances, there are two big drawbacks:

- the author may have to write a lot of content that may never get seen. For example, in Figure 25 the audience has chosen the path to end point C. This means that the content written for end points A and B is never read - unless the audience restarts the journey of course which is sometimes the goal

- when this approach is used in interactive videos, the timing of the decision points and actual choices offered are key authorial decisions. Many interactive movies don't quite work because viewers who want to "sit back" are frustrated at having to click to move forward and those who like to "sit forward" (e.g. enjoy interactive entertainment - like games) are equally frustrated at the long periods of doing nothing except laying back to watch.

Figure 26 shows a hybrid – a linear story that pretends to be branching narrative. The audience is offered a choice at the end of each scene but regardless of their decision the story branches to the same next scene. Typically this is not a recommended approach because audiences need to feel their decisions have meaning and if they replay the story or speak with others who have played the experience they'll discover that the choices are meaningless in terms of plot development. In the particular example shown, however, the interactive story is part of a two hour crisis simulation in which participants are being evaluated on their teamworking and decision-making skills – to them, under the intense time pressure of the simulation – this experience is very realistic and they never learn that their decisions haven't impacted the plot (unless they ask... and then they're disappointed).

Figure 26 Story on rails

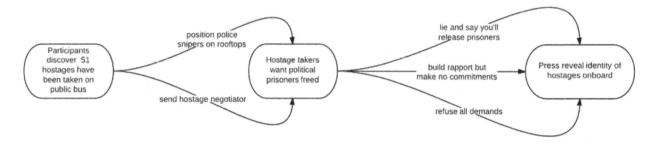

Figure 27 shows another hybrid which I've chosen to call a "dynamic" story. You'll notice that there are branches but the branches get closed down before they multiply too much. This balances the need to offer decisions that have consequences while minimizing the production of "unseen" content.

Note how the emotional state of the hostage takers is tracked and this affects how the story is told. In the opening scene they are nervous but in one path a bungled attempt to kill them with a sniper leaves them hostile. Their mood is carried into the last seen shown here and will affect how they communicate with players.

Figure 27 Dynamic story

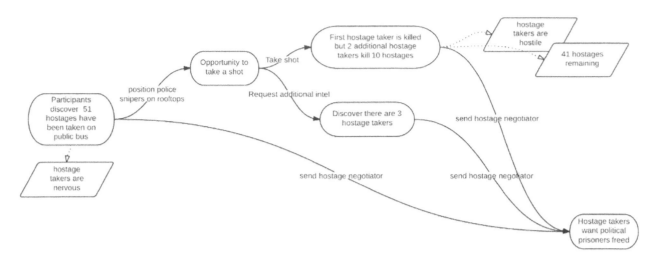

Of particular interest to transmedia storytellers is the "open storyworld" as shown in Figure 28. In the open storyworld, characters, things and places hold information that the audience must discover through investigation or exploration. The large dots in my illustration are those entities that the audience can investigate and the smaller dots represent the information held.

As the audience talks with characters or visits locations so they uncover another piece of the story.

Figure 28 Open storyworld

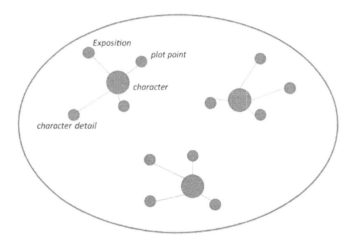

The open storyworld is often described as "non-linear storytelling" because the audience is free to explore those entities in any order - meaning that there isn't a single linear sequence or order that the audience has to follow. However, the audience' experience of the story is always linear because at this time of writing, time only flows in one direction (at least for storytellers not working at subatomic levels). So regardless of how we encounter the pieces of the story our experience is always linear. This has caused

Janet Murray to coin the term "multi-sequential" meaning that there are multiple linear sequences the audience can experience. I like this term a lot and often use it but "open storyworld" is a more familiar term which is why I've chosen it here.

This multi-sequential or open storyworld type of storytelling is particularly well suited to alternate reality games (ARGs) and location-based stories because it allows for self-guided exploration of places (virtual online or real world) and for transmedia storytelling where the open storyworld might be layered over a traditional linear narrative.

Figure 29 shows how an open storyworld can be used to create engagement between episodes of a TV series or webseries. Rather than have the audience wait a week for the next episode they can explore the open storyworld at their own pace. Even if someone watches all the episodes back-to-back the open storyworld experience will still be valid... although future video episodes might contain plot spoilers for the open storyworld if it's intended to play between episodes.

Figure 29 Open storyworld with linear media

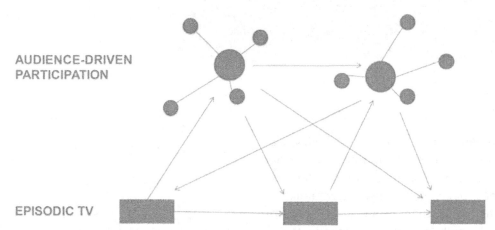

AUDIENCE-DRIVEN
PARTICIPATION

EPISODIC TV

One way to imagine this structure is as the audience being a passenger on a train from London to Manchester (See Figure 30). With linear storytelling the passenger doesn't get to move around the carriages – he's strapped to a seat and will experience the journey the same way as everyone else. With participatory storytelling – using the open world approach described above – the passenger is free to roam around the carriages. The passenger can't derail the train – it's always going to arrive in Manchester - but we've provided scope for passengers to talk to other passengers, to look out the window from different vantage points and maybe talk with characters at the time of their choosing.

Figure 30 Participatory storytelling

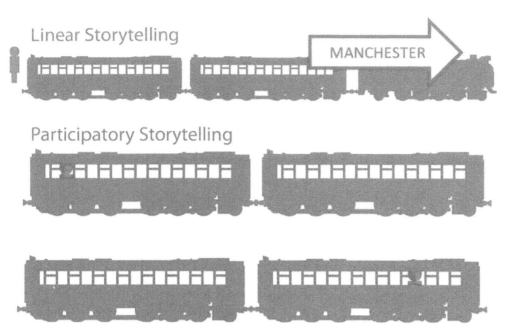

2.5 STORYWORLDS

A storyworld is the fabric of details that make a story believable. When there is a story set somewhere contemporary and familiar we tend not to notice the storyworld: we take it for granted... it's just kind of *there*. When the story is set somewhere unfamiliar, like Hogwarts or Mars or the jungle, then the storyworld is more evident – in the costumes, the architecture, the language, the props and so on.

Figure 31 Story vs Storyworld

Storyworlds are most noticeable and most important when there are many stories told about the same characters or places or objects or time period. This is because the storyworld provides the foundation to support the stories. Mark J.P Wolf says in his excellent book *Building Imaginary Worlds: The Theory and History of Subcreation*:

> "Worlds, unlike stories, need not rely on narrative structures, though stories are always dependent on the worlds in which they take place. Worlds extend beyond the stories that occur in them, inviting speculation and exploration through imaginative means"

Figure 31 illustrates multiple stories inside a storyworld with stories connected by possible narrative threads.

The storyworld then isn't a story but it holds evidence of stories and the elements from which stories are made. Imagine excavating a garden and finding broken clay pipes and coins: there's no plot here but our minds want to find significance in these items and we speculate why the pipes & coins are here, who might have used them, when did they leave them. Maybe they imply a race of people or class of society… all of which we hope will have more significance when we read a story from this storyworld or discover more artefacts.

Figure 32 is an original illustration based on the ideas in Mark J.P. Wolf's book. We see a wide range of possible elements that make up a storyworld and how these elements infuse the stories and other "non-narrative touchpoints": these are objects or experiences that reveal the storyworld but need not in themselves be part of a narrative. For example maps, excavated bones, broadcasts from a radio station, Tweets from a civic institution: they reveal the world's values and history and geography but don't necessarily deliver plot.   When working on large storyworlds, writers will create a "storyworld bible" to document all these aspects of the world but maybe only some aspects of the total world will be revealed in any single story.

Two fascinating points made by Mark in his book are:

- the more distant a world is from the audience' experience so the easier it is to create belief in the world. This is because the audience has no prior knowledge with which to consciously or subconsciously disprove what the writer is communicating. I believe this even holds true for the storyworlds of *The Godfather* and *James Bond* – I have no more personal experience of these worlds than of *Star Wars*

- the storyworld is often separated from our experience of the real world[19] by a portal of some kind which serves to create a boundary between the two. This could be a secret doorway, a narrow passage way, an ocean or maybe a specific time of day or night – anything that makes the storyworld seem less likely that we've experienced it in person.

_____

[19] In his book, Wolf explains why he prefers to use the terms Primary World (i.e. the real world) and Secondary World (i.e. a fictional world) which can be more accurate descriptions.

Figure 32 Elements of a Storyworld

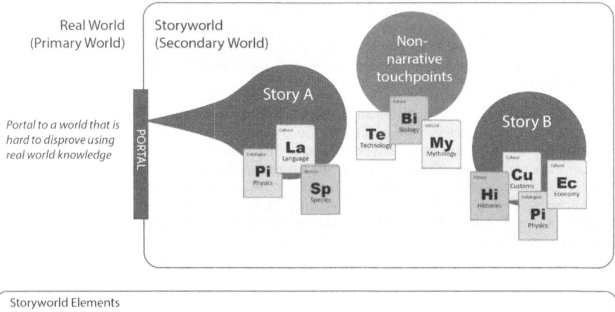

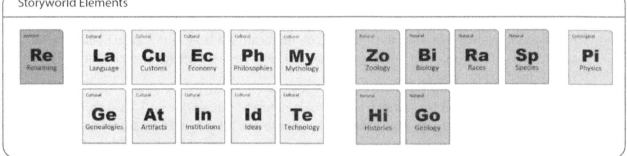

2.5.1 NARRATIVE SPACE

A story can be thought of as one implementation of the world of the story among many potential implementations (see Figure 31). I guess you might think of story as one plot line and associated characters from a world of many plots, subplots, and characters and so on – I've called this a single "narrative space". Figure 33 illustrates how an author might take a single narrative space (one story) and develop it into additional narrative spaces (new stories).

Figure 33 Narrative Space

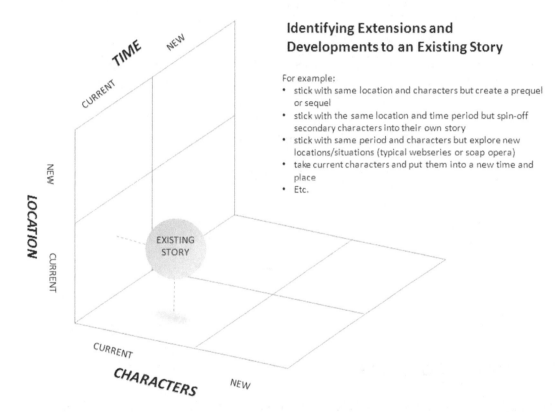

Identifying Extensions and Developments to an Existing Story

For example:
- stick with same location and characters but create a prequel or sequel
- stick with the same location and time period but spin-off secondary characters into their own story
- stick with same period and characters but explore new locations/situations (typical webseries or soap opera)
- take current characters and put them into a new time and place
- Etc.

Whether you create a storyworld bible or just write a story is really dependent on your inspiration and resources.

With Parasites (Figure 34) I started with the storyworld because I had a premise that I wanted to explore and a few ideas about a possible plot and nothing else very well developed. With Lowlifes we started with a format ("*episodic content such as blog posts, web video series and ebook*") and built out the storyworld after we had the ebook story developed. Note that given the size of the project we never did develop a story bible because I felt it was just overhead for the two of us.

Figure 34 Initial Idea Creation for Parasites

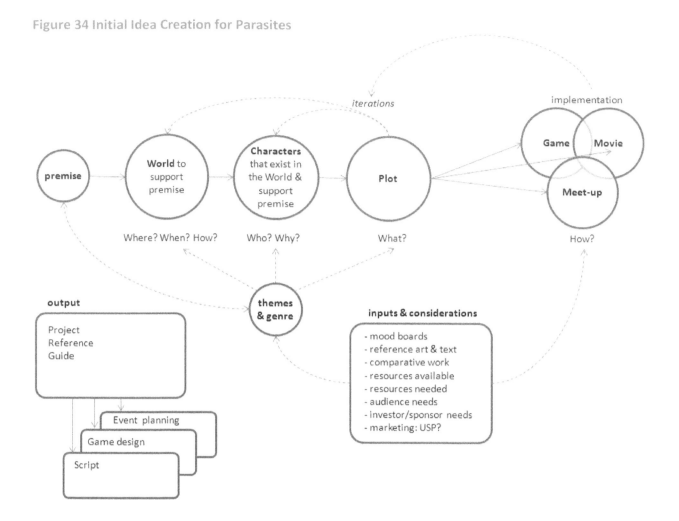

2.6   THE ACTIVE CREATION OF BELIEF

A phrase that many readers will be familiar with is "the suspension of disbelief". But a better phrase for transmedia storytellers (from Janet Murray) is "the active creation of belief". Why? Because it leads to better design decisions.

As storytellers our job is to fire the imagination. We only need provide the audience with enough information to allow them to maintain their belief in the storyworld. This is quite a different paradigm to having to provide enough information to pretend it's real. But we also have to prevent discontinuities and disturbances that would spoil the active creation of belief.

Take Disneyland for example. We know that Mickey and Minnie are not real but we want to believe in them. In Disney's theme parks, after guests have entered through the portal into the park, all the views are carefully designed and constructed to avoid anyone ever seeing the real world outside. It's important to allow imagination to work without disruption.

There is also another benefit to thinking this way: we can give the audience instructions. Instructions on how to behave, how to navigate their journey, what they're letting themselves in for, where to go if they need help and how they'll track progress. These are all important pieces of information that are needed for games and theme parks and other unfamiliar domains yet have been missing from many transmedia stories because the authors believed that to provide them would prevent suspension of disbelief. Now, thinking in terms of the active creation of belief, we can provide this very necessary and vital information in a way that enhances the experience and inspires the audience' imagination.

Providing audiences with instructions allows you another benefit – you can invite them to wear costumes. Other audience members are as much a part of the environment as the walls and props so if you can get them to dress up it can considerably enhance the experience. This is something that the British company Secret Cinema seem to be quite strict on. Figure 35 shows my wife and our friends with me wearing costumes to help recreate 1955 on the back lot of the London Olympic stadium in 2014 for Secret Cinema's *Back to the Future* experience.

Figure 35 Back to the Future – your author and friends dressed for 1955

Costumes and darkness were also key to Hal Hefner's live experience in the format of a cyber punk party for his storyworld *Unthinkable Complexity*[20]. The darkness helped obscure out-of-world distractions which

_____

[20] http://cyberpunkevent.tumblr.com/

was then maximized with many people in costume, actors and guests LARPing (live action role-playing) and many in-world artefacts left of tables such as documents, flyers and the fetus-in-jar lamp shown in Figure 36.

Figure 36 Fetus in a jar from *Unthinkable Complexity*

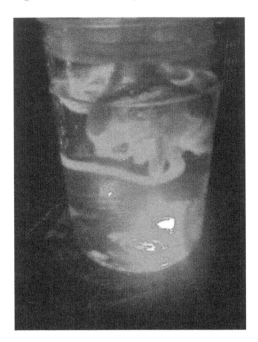

Figure 37 is a diagram I created from Hannah Rocha-Leite's graduate dissertation[21] in which she explores the research into what creates an immersive experience. It highlights the importance of providing the right cues and consistent cues to help the audience maintain belief. To summarize the diagram, it says that to create an immersive experience we must provide the audience with things to do (tactic), a reason for doing them (goal), a story to join the dots (narrative) and control the environment (space).

Space can be the most problematic to control of course – especially if it's public space - and also controlling the portal or boundary between the real world and the fictional world.

Compare, for example, the work of Secret Cinema and Punchdrunk. Secret Cinema experiences usually start out in the street around the entrance to the carefully selected building (the location selection for the last two events I've been has been spot on and I'm beginning to believe that they must find the location first and then ask what experience can we create around the place). It's as though the fictional world is spilling out into the street – there's a blurry boundary between fact and fiction. With Punchdrunk, I leave the street (where there is no evidence of what awaits) and then zigzag through a dark corridor or up an elevator. It's a kind of diver's pressure chamber that allows time for my mind and body to "normalize" to

---

[21] https://www.academia.edu/7276866/Hannah_Rocha-Leite_N0385386_BA_Hons_Theatre_Design_THTR30070_Immersion_and_Space_A_Formula_for_Spatial_Presence

the fictional world and I feel like I'm leaving the real world behind.

Figure 37 Immersion and space

Space
Control the environment to avoid incongruent cues and create congruent ones – visual and other senses

Tactics
Give the audience something to do, something to solve, something interactive

Goals
Create a mission or purpose so that the audience sees the reason in the tactics (e.g. as they move from location to location)

Narrative
Use a story to deliver entertain, engage and inform

For Canal+ we designed several live experiences in which the world of Game of Thrones (Season 4) was brought to Spain[22]. Our fictional character, Edwyck, was to meet fans in the real world – in high streets and plazas and cinemas. But seeing a guy in costume doesn't make an immersive experience! So one of our proposals was to erect a tent that looked like it belonged in that world and anyone wishing to meet Edwyck could step through the tent door to meet him. Hence our characters was "protected" from modern distractions like cars, neon lights etc. and the doorway provided a portal from the real to the fictional. Other ideas we proposed used pubs – a much better environment because we could convert them into medieval taverns. Using the pub sound system we could play our own fictional soundtrack to create the right atmosphere, we could use decorations and potentially even smells.

---

[22] Season 5 was actually shot in Spain!

3   PROJECT ORGANIZATION

Most of this book is about storytelling and experience design; this section is about organizing to do it. That is:

- Creating an organizational framework
- Creating your team
- Documenting your project

3.1   THE ORGANIZATIONAL FRAMEWORK

My particular area of interest in transmedia for the past 4 years has been the creation of persistent interactive storyworlds. That is, alternative realities that are *always* around us, not just for several weeks. To do this requires not just the technology my team and I have developed[23] but also methods, procedures, terminology, documentation and an organization. It's like inventing the motion picture camera and then having to develop the notion of movie scripts, production schedules, production teams and so on. Without the team and procedures the camera sits in the corner.

Figure 38 illustrates the understanding that underpinning every storyworld is an organization creating, organizing and delivering it. For example Ubiosoft could be the organization, Assassins Creed the storyworld and there are many executions of that storyworld from the console game to books to social games and so on. An "execution[24]", then, is an embodiment of the storyworld that can be delivered to the audience as something physical, digital or experiential.

The organization performs several functions and while I'm not attempting here to describe the full operations of a company, these functions ought to highlight the aspects of an experience that need to be cover by you and your team:

Commercial	taking care of revenue and costs (such as finance, sales and marketing)
Legal	making sure the project stays on the right side of the law
Operations	managing the ongoing experience from day-to-day (often divided into "front office" which deals with customers and "back office" which handles everything

---

[23] http://www.conducttr.com

[24] You may find it useful to think of an execution as a particular project.

else)

Delivery   getting a project (i.e. an execution of the storyworld) implemented and launched

Editorial   managing the story and experience design

Technological implementing and developing the technical side of the solution

Figure 38 Organizing for participatory worlds

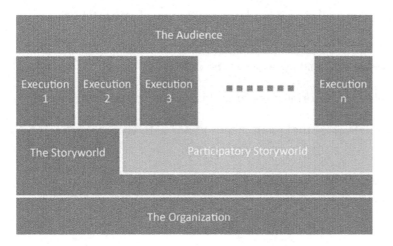

3.2   THE TEAM

To deliver a project you need a good team. There's certainly nothing to stop anyone from working alone and delivering everything but it can require a lot of skills. For example, for a recent proposal I divided the work into the following key areas:

- Management & operations
    - Project Management
    - Transmedia Producing
    - Community Management
- Creative
    - Experience Design
    - Writing
    - Concept Art & Graphics
- Technology
    - Creative Technology
    - Technical Architecture
    - Web Development
    - Conducttr Implementation

I didn't use specific job titles because in our company certain people will often perform multiple roles and some functions are shared. While we are each given responsibilities, it's very much a collaborative team-based approach. Note too that missing from the list are production roles for shooting videos, for example, and functions like social media, marketing and adverting etc. because these roles were to be performed by others.

From my experience I believe there are many 2 and 3-people teams sharing these functions, usually broadly split between "creative" and "technical" or creative/technical/management but again very collaborative and lots of cross-working.

For the first version of this book I created the following list of job roles and titles which may still be helpful:

- Executive Producer - financials and overall financial project success

- Visionary/ Creative Director - responsible for ensuring a coherent vision and coherent storyworld

- Transmedia Producer - responsible for delivering the vision; negotiations with and acquisition of crew & vendors

- Experience Designer - responsible for designing (and possibly implementing) the audience experience

- Head Writer/ Creative Director - responsible for the editorial process of ensuring continuity of story, tone & voice across all the platforms

- Writer - responsible for writing the storyworld or stories within it

- For each platform

    o Platform Producer

    o Writer

    o Creative Director

    o Various crew depending on the platform ranging from camera crew & costume designers through to software developers, runners, comic book artist and so on

- Marketing Manager/Producer

- Community Manager

- Outside agencies: lawyers, digital/interactive, PR, seeding

3.3   THE PROJECT PLAN

Figure 39 presents a four-stage workflow for creating a transmedia project.

The process works like this:

- Define what it is you're trying to achieve. *What's your objective* in creating this experience?

- Develop your ideas further and create a skeleton, a strawman, a framework of the experience. What does this experience look like?

- Design the experience in detail and document how each aspect will be implemented

- Deliver the experience to your audience.

Figure 39 Transmedia Project Workflow

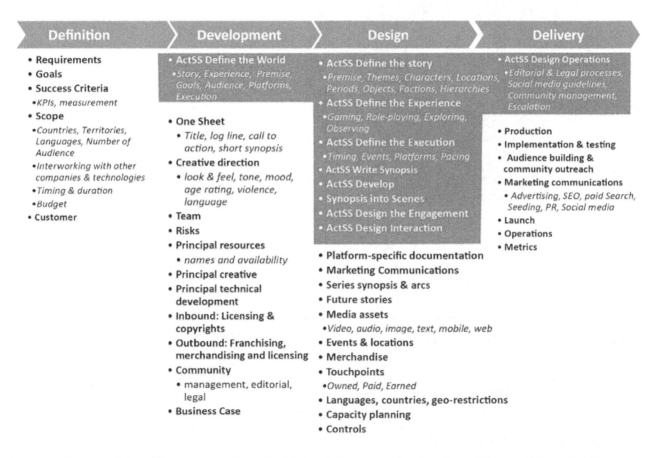

Iteration is a word that I'll use many times in this book because I don't believe it's possible to develop a project in a single linear pass. It's important at each stage to look ahead and loop back. The strength of this workflow is that it shows each stage taking the design of the experience to the next level. In practice however, projects are rarely developed in this linear fashion.

Personal projects will start with the seed of an idea, commercial projects will start with an objective and with both you're likely want to develop ideas before going into details about who's on the team and how it'll be pitched. Figure 40 shows how the creator starts with requirements and loops through the different stages adding detail and addressing practicalities.

Figure 40 Iterative workflow for the development of a transmedia project

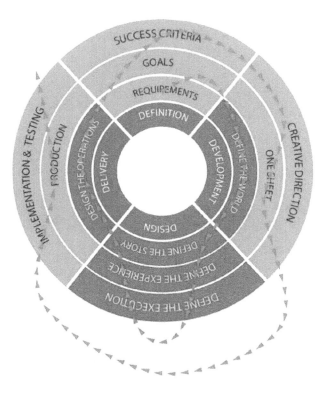

3.4   GOAL SETTING

You're likely coming at a project from one of two directions:

- artistic project
- commercial project.

3.4.1   ARTISTIC PROJECTS

You might think that a personal creative project doesn't need any goals and you could be right. However, I've seen many more projects start than get completed and it's usually because the creator runs out of enthusiasm and drive. Therefore, I strongly recommend that you set yourself some SMART goals: **S**pecific, **M**easurable, **A**ttainable, **R**ealistic and **T**imely. That is, be pragmatic and specific about what you can achieve with the resources you have.

Goals might include, given a definite timeframe: artistic challenges you set for yourself, raising finance, raising your personal profile, gaining more Twitter followers and so on. Let's consider some examples.

Example 1: "By Sept 2014 I want to have created a 40,000 word ebook about a mutant bounty hunter that sells 4000 copies for $2.99". You might be thinking "writing an ebook isn't transmedia storytelling" - and you're right - but this goal focuses on the revenue model. If we assume the creator only sees 70% of the $2.99 retail price then the total revenue is just over $8,000. That's not enough money to give up the day job and it helps to focus the mind on the investment (time and money) and social media storytelling that will be required to sell 4000 copies. And that's where, in this example at least, the transmedia storytelling comes in: how can I get the ebook story to live beyond the ebook so that it spreads through social networks and fans advocate for it?

Example 2: "By Dec 2013, I want to enable disadvantaged teens to create street games in their local area by delivering a 'transmedia toolkit' to 10 national inner-city community centers".

3.4.2 SCOPE

The principal job of the scope is to create some boundaries. Look ahead to the Development, Design and Delivery stage issues and go through the list to see what you need to address here.

For example, you might say the project will only be in English language, location-based games will be limited to San Francisco although online content will be available internationally and no new technology will be developed.

The idea is that you communicate the ambitions of the project, and address the implications of crewing and budgeting, without yet having to design the whole experience in detail.

3.4.3 SUCCESS CRITERIA

In Goals you set yourself some targets; here you explain how you'll recognize when those goals have been achieved.

Note that for goals related to things like awareness and sales, there could be a number of factors that make measuring these problematic such as a lag or continued effect after the project has wrapped or the impact of other events outside your control such as economic collapse, a disappointing product (if it's a new product launch) and so on. Hence try to specific about what tools and metrics you'll use.

3.4.4   BUDGET

How much does it cost to make a feature-length movie? $50,000? $3million? $240million? The answer is that you could create a movie for any amount of money so it's usually a case of either fitting a project to the money available or setting yourself a certain level of ambition and designing to that. Whatever your budget you'll always say it's not enough.

Line items you'll need to consider if you plan to make a profit are:

- a cost breakdown of the project by platform and by cost type (capital costs and operating costs)

- a revenue breakdown of the project by source (sponsorship, grants, direct finance, pre-sales, sales and so on)

- break-even analysis (the point at which the total net revenue matches the total costs).

Costs typically fall into the team structure given in 3.2 plus some additional items:

- Professional fees (project management, design, implementation, operation)
- Production costs (shooting, printing, editing etc)
- Hosting & license fees
- Travel & accommodation

3.4.5   REVENUE MODEL

The business model explains how you are going to pay for the project. You have three primary choices:

- Sponsored (e.g. free to Audience) - here the project is paid for by the author (self-funded) or by a 3rd party such as a brand (advertising, product placement, branded entertainment) or by benefactors (crowdfunded, arts endowment)

- Audience-pays - purchase of content through paid downloads, physical product, subscriptions or membership

- Freemium - mix of Sponsored and Audience-paid content that may change over time.

Given the importance of financing, I've given it its own section (See Section 8) but here I wanted to look at how you might decide what the best business model for your project is:

- Look at your audience – what do they buy and how do they buy?

- Look at the platforms you're considering – which platforms support the sponsored approach (e.g. social and easily shared) and which support the paid?

Figure 41 illustrates how different platforms lend themselves to different financing methods. I originally created the graphic for a presentation to the Music Business School[25] in London but it's possible to use the same axes and position other platforms more relevant to your project.

Figure 41 Multi-platform Strategy (Music example)

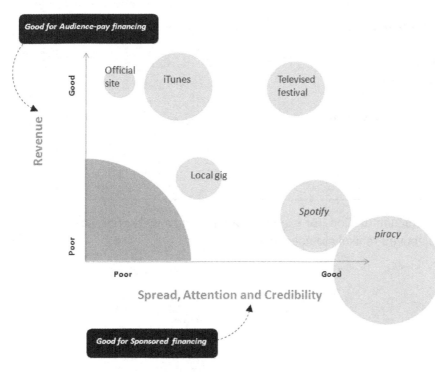

Remember to iterate back to the story and this time think about the experience in terms of the business model. How can you develop your story and platforms to better suit the business model?

3.5 COMMERCIAL PROJECTS

If you're creating a project for a client then Ogilvy's *Branded Entertainment Assessment Model*™ is an excellent place to start. It identifies three primary considerations: reach, preference and action. The model acknowledges that all three of the following need to work together but that only one should be the main focus. In the following list the lines in bold are directly from Ogilvy and the other suggestions I've added:

- **Reach**
    - Increase awareness
    - Reinforce positioning
    - Generate press & word-of-mouth

---

[25] http://musicbusinessschool.co.uk/

- **Preference**
  - Ensure desired perception of brand
  - Bring to life boring and undifferentiated products
  - Generate word-of-mouth for low-involvement products
  - (re)Build brand image
  - Re-position against competitors
- **Action**
  - Generate product trial
  - Increase consumer advocacy
  - Generate sales
  - Generate opt-in (e.g. loyalty program)

3.6 DOCUMENTATION

In addition to any specific production documentation (for example for shooting a webseries, say) the key documentation for a transmedia project you're likely to need are:

- The Proposal
- The One Sheet
- The Story Bible
- The Participation Bible
- A Platform Chart
- Scene chart
- User Journey Diagrams

3.6.1 THE PROPOSAL

A proposal document will likely have the following sections:

- Summary (The headlines) - this is a short pitch of what you propose to do
- Background – why is this project necessary? What problem does it solve?
- Proposal body – what, when and where?
- Team – who's working on this and why
- Pricing – how much and how is it paid?

3.6.1.1 THE HEADLINES

Not only is it important to be able to pitch your project quickly and simply but I feel that transmedia projects can very quickly become unwieldy and possibly unnecessarily complex. Working on the headlines first puts some boundaries on the project and helps to focus the mind on what you're trying to achieve.

I usually spend a lot of time on this area trying to boil down an idea into something that's easy to understand by someone unfamiliar with transmedia jargon.

The headlines of your story-experience will include:

- **short synopsis** - what happens?

- **player goal** – what is the audience expected to do?

- **high concept** - how does the story play put across platforms?   The term "high concept" is used a lot in the movie world and I've borrowed it because I think it's a good starting place: It's a paragraph that easily communicates your project .

- **premise** - what are you trying to say? This is the point-of-view of the story

- **theme** - what's the recurrent motif or unifying idea that holds everything together? Try to get this to a single word like "obsession" or "temptation" or "courage"

- **genre** - what audience is going to like this project?

Here's an example for my project Lowlifes:

Short synopsis	*Lowlifes tells the fictional story of a drug-addicted San Francisco homicide detective, his ex-wife and the private eye she's hired to spy on him*
Player goal	*Find a murderer by interacting with (non-player) characters via SMS and email*
High concept	*One story told over three platforms – a novella, a web series and a blog. Each platform represents one of three principal characters*
Premise	*Don't judge a book by its cover*
Theme	*Home*
Genre	*Crime*

3.6.2   THE ONE SHEET

The "one sheet" is an idea I took from the movie business where it refers to a single page that communicates (sells) the most important things about a project.

Section 2.1.2 explains how to create this one sheet but it's not something I'd ever show to someone unfamiliar with transmedia storytelling. It's a great way to communicate a project but only those who know what they're looking at – a bit like an Xray!

3.6.3 THE STORY BIBLE

If you're intending for anyone to collaborate on the project – be it the audience, franchisees, subcontractors or whoever – then documenting the storyworld will have a greater significance because it's the primary reference the ensures everyone is "in canon".   The word "canon" refers to a set of rules, beliefs, principles, characters, events and so on that are true to the storyworld. Everyone creating content for the storyworld ought to be in canon or else the inconsistencies will create dissatisfaction for audiences because the stories won't ring true. Also, not providing a clear path for collaboration will create problems for you developing your own stories in this world.

Having said this, many fans get satisfaction from creating and consuming fan fiction precisely because it's "out of canon" – it's in a parallel fictional reality to the "authorized" storyworld. Nevertheless one benefit of creating the bible is to distinguish what is part of the world and what is not... although defining what's not part of the world will actually make it part of a larger world... urggh! Enough.

In developing a world you want to create a world that's big enough to give you plenty of scope for multiple stories and characters. Even if you'll only implement a fraction of that world in the first instance, you're laying the ground work for future implementations: series of movies, games, books and so on. I don't believe that a "big enough" world means you need an encyclopedic universe of thousands of characters and locations, I'm saying just don't write yourself into a corner.

The output from this process is often referred to as a "Bible" – it's the holy source that all should refer to and adhere to.

Figure 42 The Storyworld Bible

1. Storyworld (Mythos)
    a. Characters and factions
    b. Timeline – events, wars, treaties
    c. Topography & maps - locations/states/cities
    d. Population
    e. Culture
    f. Religion
    g. Language
    h. Economy
    i. Science & Technology (& Magic)
2. Series synopsis and arcs
3. Future stories

There's a great wiki, an online tool and community for developing storyworlds at ConWorld[26] and I'd also

---

[26] http://conworld.wikia.com/wiki/Main_Page

recommend checking out Worldbuilding[27] on Wikipedia.

Note that the bible has only covered the story – not the experience. You can still download a document template I created called the Project Reference Document[28].

3.6.4 THE PARTICIPATION BIBLE

Please see Section 4.1

3.6.5 THE PLATFORM CHART

The platform chart provides an overview of the relative timings of the different platforms in your experience. In the first version of this book I shared my thinking and experiments with various approaches to finding a single diagram that would communicate the whole complexity of a project. In the end I abandoned this approach in favor of two primary documents – the platform chart and the audience/user journey diagram.

There's an excellent presentation from Christy Dena[29] in which she identifies some key requirements for transmedia documentation:

- indicate which part of the story is told by which media

- indicate the timing of each element

- indicate how the audience traverses the media (what's the call to action?)

- indicate what the audience actually sees and does

- take account of the possibility for "non-linear traversal" through the story

- provide continuity across developers (who may be working on different media assets)

Christy also references music notation and says that it would be nice to present a transmedia project in this way so that someone could see the beauty of it at a glance.

During the writing of the first version of this book I'd been looking at this approach myself and I'm not the first. I knew that Mike Figgis (who is a composer as well as a director) worked on Timecode[30] using a kind of music notation to present and explain his ideas for four stories would be told simultaneously in real-

---

[27] http://en.wikipedia.org/wiki/Worldbuilding
[28] http://www.slideshare.net/ZenFilms/transmedia-project-reference-guide-bible
[29] http://www.slideshare.net/christydena/lessons-learned-in-crossmedia
[30] http://www.red-mullet.com/home.html

time. And it's with his kind permission that I'm able to reproduce an example here.   I'd encourage you to check out the movie and the rest of the script.

Figure 43 Mike Figgis' *Timecode*: script page

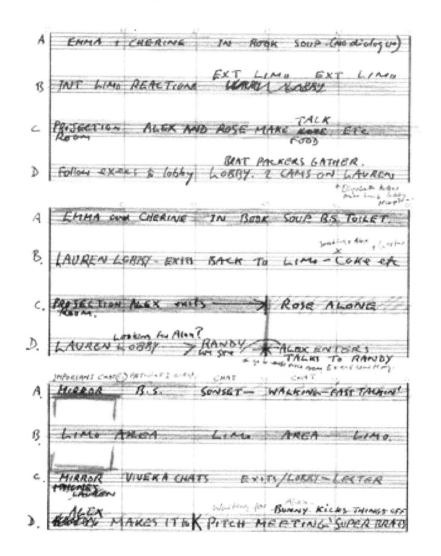

Figure 44 shows Steve Peter's (No Mimes Media) International Mimes Academy ARG as a platform chart. Note that it's the platforms that take precedence in this diagram and it's actually tricky to clearly see the audience' journey. It is useful though for highlighting the platforms used and how prevalent they are in the experience.

Figure 44 Documentation for International Mimes Academy Mini-ARG

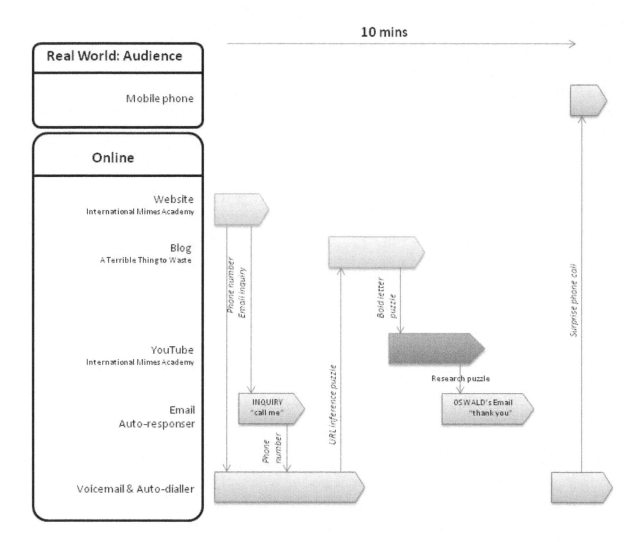

What's good about this approach is that it hits a lot of the goals desired by Christy Dena:

- indicate which part of the story is told by which media

- indicate the timing of each element

- indicate how the audience traverses the media (what's the call to action?)

Separating out the media like this is particularly useful if it's being created by partners or collaborators: it shows what has to be created and how it relates to other media. The colored vectors represent the different platforms and the thin arrows between them document the calls-to-action or bridges between the platforms.

The one "exception" that I made for this documentation is the inclusion of the final phone call. Typically I wouldn't' include the audience in the diagram but as it's a concluding part of this experience it felt incomplete without it.

Ultimately it was the complications of adding those smaller action arrows that cross between platforms that was the downfall of this approach and it was the simplicity of Figure 45 - which shows the quick sketch I did for Heroes of the North[31] - that lead me to simplify the platform chart to that showed in Figure 46 for the Mask of the Red Death. All the zigzagging arrows are gone and the chart simply shows the timing between platforms.

Figure 45 Platform Chart for Heroes of the North ARG (initial sketch)

Narrative Act	WEEK 1 Issue Warnings	WEEK 2 Clues Emerge	WEEK 3 All Seems Lost	WEEK 4 Climax
Game Arc	Establish primary threat: Medusa will release neutron bomb to wipe out all the city's electronics. They don't say where or when.	Quests: 1. Find location 2. Find deadline 3. Gather decoder (puzzle pieces) 4. Moral choices?	Clues have all existing clues lead to dead-ends. Heroes are despondent. Thursday: A NEW LEAD! New Hope! Hero's have found some event will happen at start of Week 4 to reveal deadline.	Rapid pace of clues – one per day. The net closes in. More international involvement
Publicity	Get as many local people as possible. Local media & traditional press Flyers, hand-outs etc.			Maximum people anywhere Maximum online & social media activity
Player Success	Needs a handout from the first week of activity – that makes sure it's a local person who gets the prize 😊		Needs a handout from the first week of activity – that makes sure it's a local person who gets the prize	Special physical puzzle pieces used to defuse the bomb must be collected around town.
ONLINE				Speculation online about what the pieces might be. The handout as a CODE that shows correct ordering of the pieces! Final tip-off is given at 6am on morning of party
Twitter & RSS crisis feeds		VILLAIN sites found?		Those arriving at scene must solve the Chinese puzzle with the physical pieces and fit them into the bomb to defuse it!
CDO	Sign-up page: WANTED posters Community upload area for sightings	HEROES clarify quests in response to VILLAINS	Countdown begins	Have the baddies and Heroes arrive to fight on the scene while the fans try to solve the puzzle! Have a "fan" as insider filming everything.
New Felquists Medusa		VILLAINS come out of hidding and reveal their aims (and hence quests)		
REAL WOLRD				
Public Spaces	Go to shopping malls and handout calls for help! Heroes need your support! Have you see this VILLAIN?			
Hidden Locations "Drop-boxes"			Digital artifacts: use old tech too like a floppy disc!	Physical pieces left around
Launch Party (LOCATION OF BOMB!)				★

31   http://www.heroesofthenorth.com/

Figure 46 Platform chart for *Mask of the Red Death*

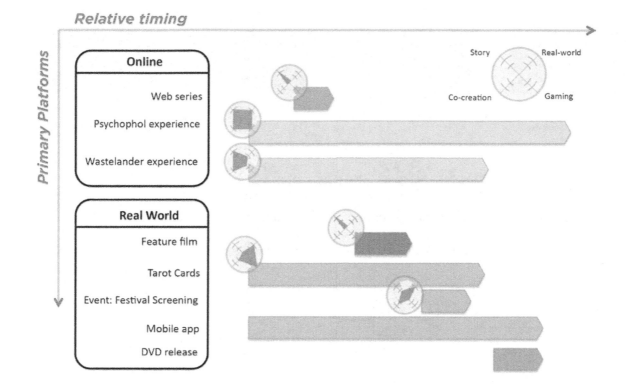

3.6.6 SCENE CHART

Participatory stories require the audience to do something to unlock the story. The "scene chart" is a high-level view of how the actions taken by the audience move the story forward –with the focus predominantly on the story.

A very simple chart is given in Figure 47 where the audience needs to unlock the secret that Daniel is a millionaire and owns a security company. To get this knowledge the audience must find a series of clues.

Figure 48 gives a more complex example for a twitter-based game in which the audience must obtain some patient records. Creating and understanding these charts is explained in Section 6.

PROJECT ORGANIZATION

Figure 47 Clues to solve the first Daniel Northman quest

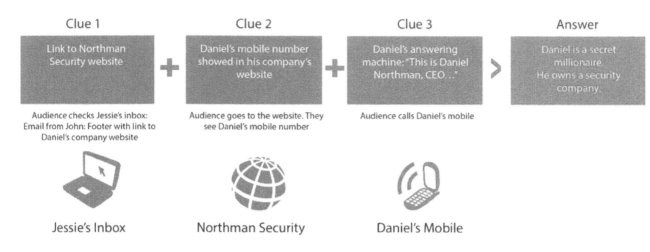

Figure 48 Scenes for the Psychophol experience (part of Mask of the Red Death)

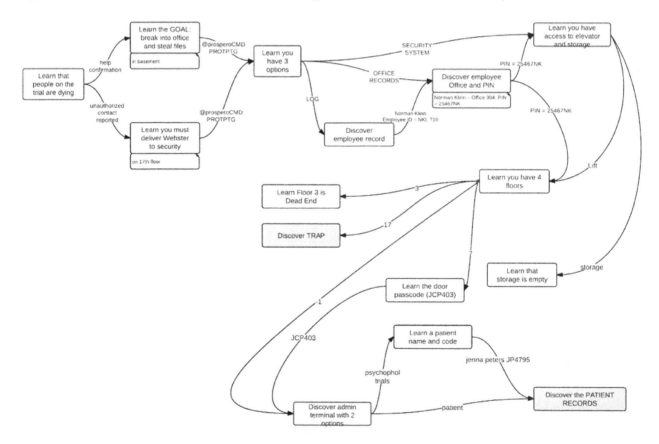

3.6.7   AUDIENCE/USER JOURNEY DIAGRAM

With the platform chart now much simplified to providing only an overview, there is still a need to show how the audience crosses between platforms. The answer was in the audience/user experience diagram.

The 10 minute ARG created by No Mimes LLC called *International Mimes Academy* remains for many a go-to demonstration of what an ARG is. If you're not already familiar with this game, you can download an explanation at the Unfiction forum[32]. The user journey diagram created by No Mimes LLC is presented in Figure 49.

This pictorial flowchart is pretty good because it shows the media and links or calls-to-action between the media and there's an implied sequence of experience (from top to bottom).

A different example is given in Figure 50 for the initial quest in the work Nataly Rios did for The Chatsfield (a storyworld developed by Alison Norrington for Harlequin Mills and Boon). The subsequent images show how we arrived at this journey: we started with the overall narrative (Figure 51) and created four quests (missions for the audience to complete) and then for each quest we created a high-level diagram of what clues were needed to complete the quest (Figure 47).

The user journey diagrams can take some time to create but they are effective in communicating how the experience unfolds.

---

[32] http://forums.unfiction.com/forums/files/mime_academy_design_handout.pdf

Figure 49 International Mime Academy Flowchart

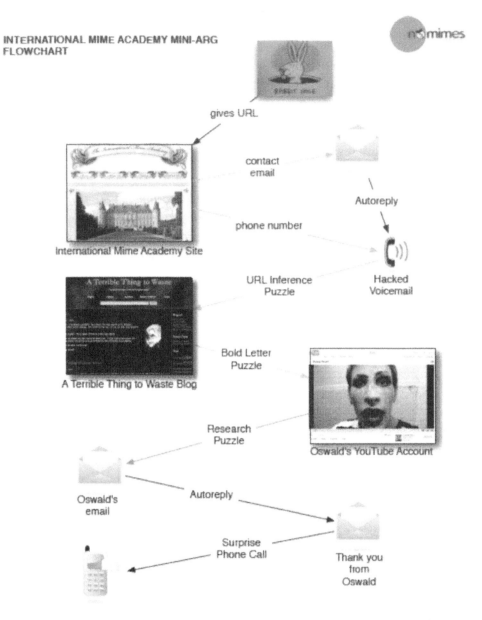

Figure 50 User Journey Diagram for Who Is Daniel Northman

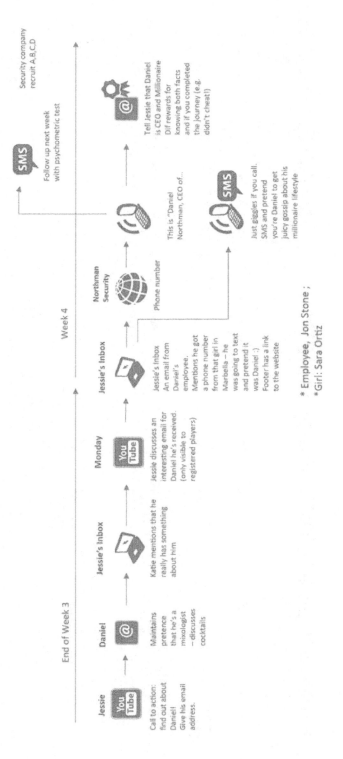

Figure 51 Developing the Daniel Northman mystery

	MAY				JUNE					JULY		
	Week 1	Week 2	Week 3	Week 4	Week 5	Week 6	Week 7	Week 8	Week 9	Week 10	Week 11	Week 12
Jessie's world	New Arrival: Daniel is the new employee working at the bar.	Who is he? Jessie wonders who Daniel really is.			Why is he working at the bar? Jessie wants to find out the real reason Daniel is at the bar.			Attraction. Jessie and Daniel get closer. Attraction grows stronger.		Revenge or Justice? Daniel struggles deciding whether to kill Matthias and revenge his father's death, or bring him to justice.		Final Decision. Jessie helps Daniel to make the right thing. He doesn't kill Matthias.
Quest		Find out who Daniel is! What's his story			Find out why is Daniel working at the hotel! What's the real reason?		Find out the right target. Who was driving that car and killed Daniel's Father?			Should Daniel kill Matthias?		
Mystery's Answer		Daniel is a secret millionaire with his own security company			Daniel wants to find his father's killer. Father was killed in hit and run 5 years ago in Spain. The search has lead Daniel to this hotel and 4 people who work or live there (4 guys at the bar)		The accident is linked to a robbery in which the 4 guys were involved. The car of the accident was used to complete the crime. Matthias was the head planner, but it is revealed that none of the guys was driving the car. Who was driving? It is discovered that the driver died, but it was Matthias who gave the order to take the fatal route, so he is responsible for the father's death.					
Audience's Action		Audience investigates who Daniel really is.			Audience investigates what is Daniel really doing at the hotel.		Audience investigates the 4 guys at the bar in order to discover who is the killer.			Audience votes to help Daniel decide whether to kill Matthias or go to the police.		

3.6.8 PRACTICAL CONSIDERATIONS FOR DOCUMENTING THE AUIDENCE JOURNEY

In addition to the creative considerations of the audience journey, there are also practical considerations that relate to operation and management. That is, we need to consider how a person will become known to the system controlling the experience and what happens to their data after the experience ends. If the experience is replayable, we need to know what are the starting conditions and what conditions or parameters must be reset.

Figure 52 shows five phases of the audience journey:

- **Setup** - this phase encompasses all the actions that take place before the audience can register. It would include, for example, the actions required to reset the experience back to the starting state if it were a repeatable experience

- **Registration** - this phase encompasses the actions required to make the audience known to the experience. For example, the audience emailing a character or using a sign-up form or texting a number. It's the first contact your experience makes with the audience.

- **Activation** - this phase is where the experience calls the audience to action. In many cases the time delay between Registration and Activation might be negligible but other times the audience might register for a period of weeks or months before the project enters a campaign period - which would then start with Activation

- **Play** - this is the main body of the experience

- **Wrap** - this phase encompasses the actions required to wrap up the experience.

Figure 52 Five phases of Audience Journey

Documentation for an interactive experience ought to identify these five phases and detail:

- People involved
- Locations, parameters, timing needed for each phase
- Any differences between first run-through and subsequent run-throughs if this is a repeatable experience
- Measurements and metrics required

4   DEVELOPING A PARTICIPATORY STORYWORLD

It could be said that storyworlds exist independently of any real-world limitations that might inhibit their successful realization: they are a purely creative invention. However, when we come to deliver the storyworld – to put it into the heads, hands and hearts of people outside our circle of family & friends – then real-world practicalities such as competition, limited resources (time, money, ability) and the need to achieve certain goals (creative, professional, social, commercial) require us to create a framework or foundation to inform the realization.

As a producer (rather than as a writer), usually I'm starting with a framework and required to develop or refine a storyworld so that the two work in harmony. This led me to develop the *Active Story System*[TM] – a methodology for creating participatory storyworlds. It's a transmedia storytelling framework that:

- is goal-oriented
- is designed for commercial & creative success
- integrates engagement, social media & content strategy.

It can be used by artists and writers as well as agency account managers, planners and creative directors. It's a way to structure and document participatory transmedia storyworlds. Other people may have developed processes for the development of storyworlds but the *Active Story System*[TM] focuses specifically on creating **active audience involvement**.

Central to *Active Story System*[TM] are two basic beliefs:

- **that content creators need to bake the marketing into the entertainment**. That is, that audience discovery, retention, engagement, social spread and word-of-mouth need to be designed at the same time as the story is written and built into the foundations of the world. This approach treats all stories as an experience that must be designed and planned for

- **that storyworlds should be participatory.** That is, that the storyworld is a living, breathing world with which the audience can interact and possibly contribute to.

4.1   THE PARTICIPATION BIBLE

One aspect that's unique about the *Active Story System*[TM] is the concept of a *participatory storyworld* – this explicitly recognizes that audience involvement needs to be encouraged and supported. This support comes in the form of policies, procedures (design and operational) and technology that needs to be documented and brought together in a cohesive way. Hence the need for a **Participation Bible** (see Figure 53) that documents:

- Goals for audience participation (commercial & creative objectives)
- Policy (for treating fans consistent with company core values)
- In-world Design (e.g. storytelling)
  - Gaming/Role-playing/Observing/Exploring
  - Platforms
  - Events
  - Timing
- Out of World Design (e.g. company policy)
  - Social media policy (communication style, crisis management)
  - Community policy (rewards, highlighting, banning, legal action)
  - Editorial policy for fan-generated content (encouraged, allowed, ignored, removed)
  - Legal policy
  - Escalation procedures

Finally, to deliver the participatory storyworld - as any number of executions (i.e. projects) - we need various pieces of documentation as shown in Figure 54. The *Active Story System^{TM}* documents relate specifically to the design of the participatory storyworld and any number of executions of that world: they are not enough alone to actually deliver the execution which still requires project-specific and platform-specific documentation.

Figure 53 The Participatory Storyworld and the Participation Bible

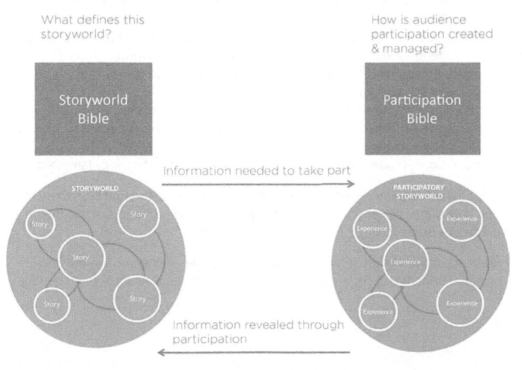

Figure 54 Documentation to deliver a participatory storyworld

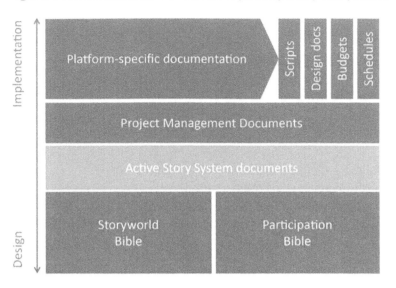

4.2   ACTIVE STORY SYSTEM™ OVERVIEW

The Active Story System™ is in two core parts or stages:

- **definition of the participatory storyworld:**
    - o   the world – agree who it's for, the goals and the underlying transmedia format
    - o   the story – identify key parts of the narrative that can be used for participation
    - o   the experiences – identify different opportunities for participation (i.e. many executions)
    - o   the execution – identify when and how the experiences will be delivered
- **design of the participatory experience(s)** (i.e. a particular execution of the storyworld):
    - o   write a synopsis for this execution/project
    - o   breakdown the synopsis into scenes (and beats)
    - o   design the engagement – why and how will people engage with this experience
    - o   design the interaction – where and how
    - o   design the operations – understand how the project will be supported once launched

An assumption here is that the *narrative* storyworld has been developed and documented elsewhere in a Story Bible (for large projects) or there is at least a short story synopsis written or that these documents will come together as work begins on designing the audience participation.

Figure 55 shows an overview of the system and how everything ties together. This section of the book explains the participatory storyworld, the rest of the book looks at the more detailed aspects of creating the executions.

Figure 55 Overview of Active Story System™

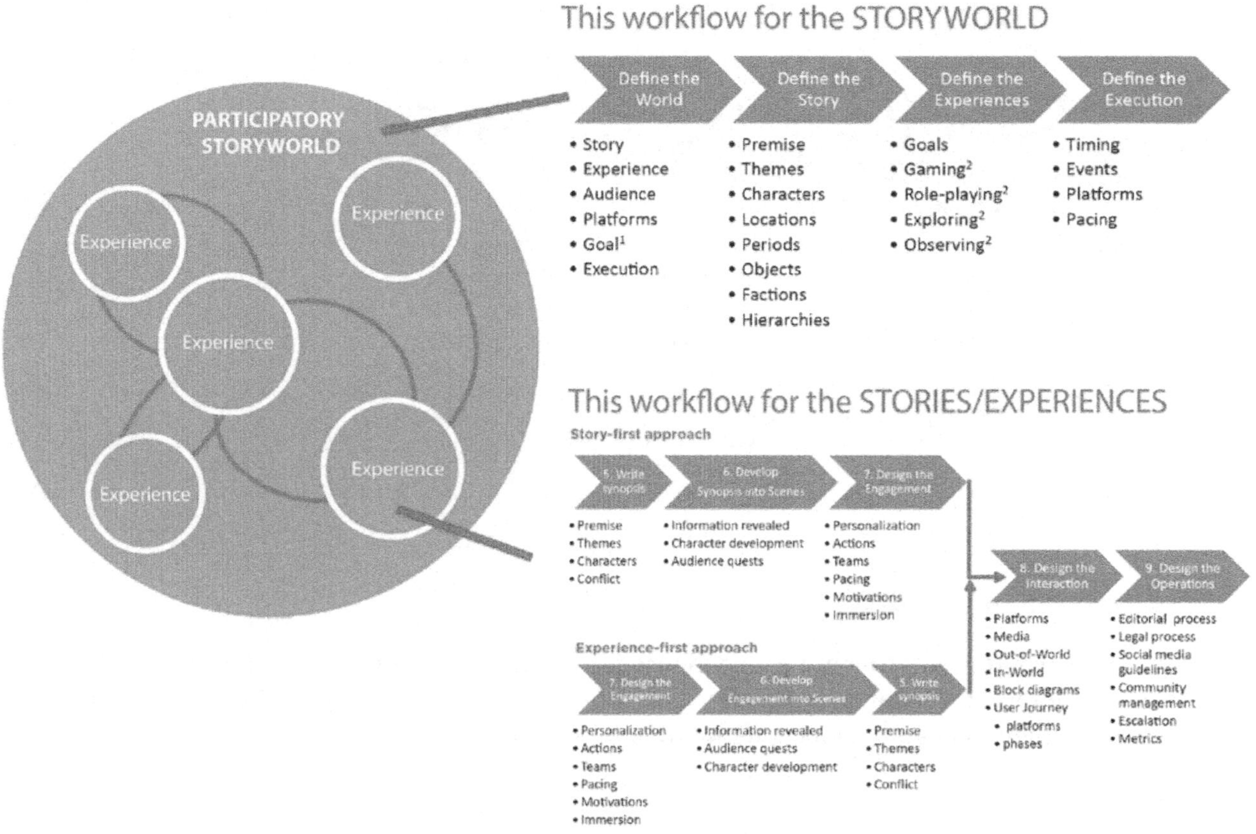

4.3 DEFINING THE STORYWORLD

This stage is in four phases (as illustrated in Figure 56):

- define the world – agree who it's for, the goals and the underlying transmedia format
- define the story – identify key parts of the narrative that can be used for participation
- define the experiences – identify different opportunities for participation (i.e. many executions)
- define the execution – identify when and how the experiences will be delivered.

Figure 56 Defining the Storyworld

4.3.1 DEFINING THE WORLD

In this phase the creator determines the experience format using the six headings identified in Figure 57. Other sections of this book deal with these areas in some detail so I won't say much more here other than to reiterate that they all need to work in harmony with each other.

Figure 57 Defining the world

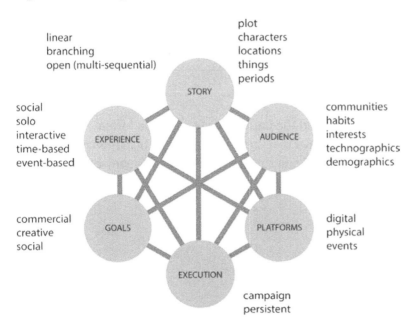

4.3.2   DEFINE THE STORY

What you are attempting to do here is pull out from the narrative key entities and elements that you might later use to either encourage participation, stimulate ideas around participation or simply to (justify?) prove a context for the actions you're requesting. The key parts to note are:

- **Premise** – What is the message the writer wants to convey? What does she believe to be true?

- **Themes** – What themes are explored?

- **Characters** – Who are the main and interesting (perhaps minor) characters?

- **Locations** - What are the main and interesting (perhaps minor) locations?

- **Periods** - Thinking of the storyworld timeline, what are the significant periods?

- **Objects** - What are the significant or iconic objects in this storyworld? (e.g. rings, goblets, sonic screwdrivers, Martini cocktails?)

- **Factions** - What are the main rivalries or tribes or sects? NB: this can help the audience identify and choose a group to belong to

- **Hierarchies** - What levels and ranks are there within the factions? NB: this can be useful for community forums and games where people can "level up" depending on activity or success.

4.3.3   DEFINE THE PARTICIPATION

Focusing on your goals and the premise, this stage involves brainstorming different opportunities for audience participation. The process provides a framework for considering four different kinds of activities:

- **Observing** - what information or questions might the audience be given to make them *think* about and reflect on the premise?

- **Exploring** - what additional information (in world and out of world) can the audience explore?

- **Gaming** - what (moral) choices might the audience be given to make them *feel* the premise?

- **Role-playing** - how will you enable the audience to role-play and create their own entertainment? In this participation type, the audience creates their own entertainment from the tools, apps, media, props (physical and digital) etc. and advice you've given them.

A key thing to remember is that all experiences must illustrate the premise. For example, if you have a premise that says "liberty must be fought for" then the experiences you design must bring the audience to the same conclusion. When you use the grid in Figure 58 be sure to have a solid understanding of the premise and use this as a constraint and focus.

Figure 58 Participation grid

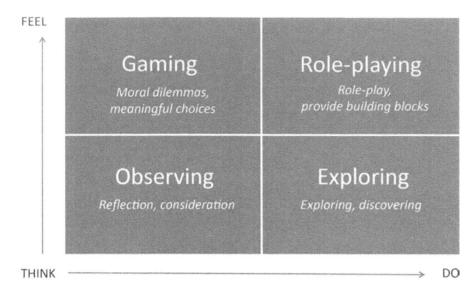

Figure 59 shows an example from a project called Mask of the Red Death. The web series is pre-recorded content so can only be gathered, the "psychophol experience" was a Twitter game and the tarot cards were to be physical cards. As physical cards, the players create their own stories using the cards as props and provocations. The "Wastelander experience" was a forum that set quests and awarded points for participation while encouraging the audience to role-play as fictional personas in the dystopian future of the movie.

Figure 59 Participation map for Mask of the Red Death

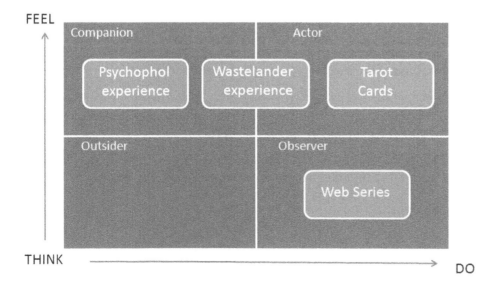

Figure 60 Tarot cards from Mask of the Red Death[33]

The above grid was the result of research I did to look at different roles for the audience and their relationship to the storyworld. For example, outside looking in ("observing") – reflecting and analyzing – or on the inside acting with autonomy ("role-playing") or walking beside a character as a companion ("gaming"). Figure 61 illustrates the initial work.

4.3.3.1 SOLO, COMMUNITY AND SINGLE PLAYER VS MULTIPLAYER

There's another dimension to the audience participation beyond which role they play - it's their relationship to and dependence on others.

---

[33] Created by Santeri Lohi at BTL Brands

I think of this audience relationship in as being in five categories:

- solo   actions taken alone and in private
- teams   groups of players working together for a shared goal
- community   single-player actions taken in public and shared with or discussed with the community
- competitive   actions taken in competition with others or with a fictional character
- collaborative   actions take in collaboration with others or with a fictional character.

Figure 62 presents a table intended to prompt ideas for the kinds of participation you might invite the audience to take part in. It's not intended to be comprehensive, just indicative. I also recommend checking out Amy Jo Kim's blog post on "social engagement verbs"[34] where she explains the limitation of Bartle player types (see Figure 68 and Figure 69) and presents her own matrix to suggest things we might invite audiences to do. I've reproduced her diagram in Figure 63.

Figure 61 Audience and Storyworld

	Feelings			Thoughts
	Inside the Storyworld			Outside the Storyworld
	Audience as Actor	**Audience as Companion**	**Audience as Observer**	**Audience as Audience**
Audience is:	Interacting to **role-play** in the fictional world		Interacting to **explore** the fictional world	Interacting **reflect** on the theme, construction
Reflecting	Reflection within the role played		Reflection within the storyworld	Reflection on premise, themes, story from outside the fiction
Acting	Interaction allows reader to create their own story		Interaction doesn't change the story but allows reader to explore	Interaction is outside the storyworld
Author should:	Provide tools & content to facilitate role-play & socializing Storyworld mythos, ethos, typos with characters, locations and objects provide building blocks for role-play.	Provide questions & quests that facilitate exploration & socializing Audience discovers the storyworld through interaction with the characters, locations & things.		Provide tools & content that complements the storyworld such as teaching aids, quizzes, polls etc. that encourages reader to reflect on the issues dealt with in the storyworld and promotes debate
		Group audience into teams/sects/roles and provide each with a unique perspective on the storyworld to encourage socializing Characters set readers challenges and conundrums.		
Social	Encourage audience to socialize in-world and in-character	Encourage audience socialize in forum & social media to find other readers in different teams/sects/roles; to find cues and clues to unlock parts of the world (e.g. to help them explore further)		Encourage audience debate the issues, themes, premise that are central to the storyworld

Figure 62 Participation-Interaction table

		Solo	Compete						Collaborate			Converse	
			Place	Time	My Best	Chars	Others	Teams	Chars	Others	Teams	Chars	Others
Private Actions	See Watch Read Click Download												
Public Actions	Vote Quiz Like Join Comment Tweet ReTweet Refer Share Chat Remix Upload Create												
	Purchase												

Figure 63 Participation opportunities for audiences

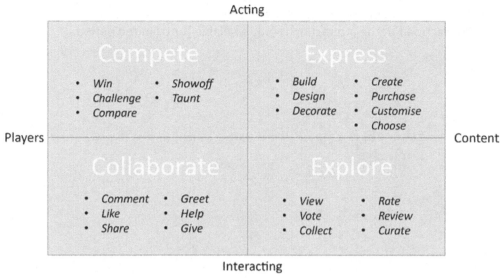

source: Amy Jo Kim

4.3.4   DEFINE THE EXECUTION

In the previous stage you will have identified a number of experiences[35]. You now have to organize these in relation to each other, to other marketing or public events (e.g. Labor Day, Christmas, and Halloween etc.) and to commercial objectives – usually there is a reason for launching the project *now* and not later. The key considerations then, are:

- **Timing** - what content and experiences will be made available and when?

- **Events** – what are the "tent pole" events or prominent dates in your calendar and how does the storyworld fit with them?

- **Platforms** – you defined the platforms in phase 1 but how do they now fit against each other

- **Pacing** – what's the release plan? How are the content and experiences going to be made available in relation to each other?

Typically, the execution will be shown as an experience timeline of the kind shown in Figure 46. This gives a broad-brush overview of the release of different experiences and how long they are to last.

It's also very useful to map the experiences on a content availability grid of the type shown in Figure 64. In

---

[35] Here I mean "experiences" in its broadest possible use to encompass books, movies, ARGs, pervasive games, interactive webseries and so on.

this grid, "interactive" experiences are those that are available all the time yet start on demand and deliver content to the audience based on their actions. In contrast, "scheduled" content is published to a campaign timeline and require no interaction from the audience. "Scheduled interactive" is content delivered through audience interaction but the interaction is only available for a limited period.

Figure 64 Content availability grid

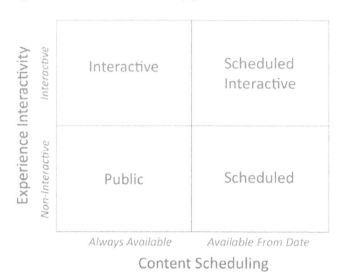

5   UNDERSTANDING THE AUDIENCE

5.1   AUDIENCES – INDENTIFYING AND UNDERSTANDING THEM

For the most part, I'm going to assume that your project is being driven by a creative idea that's dear to you rather than assume you have consumers for whom you need to find a creative idea. Regardless though, the most important point to understand is that **your audience are the ones for whom your message is relevant and resonates**.

There are two steps to recognizing your audience:

- identify who they are
- understand what turns them on

In taking these two steps you'll be able to offer the right content, to the right people and the right time.

5.2   IDENTIFYING YOUR AUDIENCE

Below is a list of considerations for scoping your audience. Going through the list below you will be able to identify (and discount) appropriate platforms, when your audience might be viewing or interacting, how big an audience you have and where you might approach them. You should do this:

- (a) through the lens of your project's themes, genre and characters
- (b) with a particular question in mind (say, regarding business models and likely touchpoints) so as to save you a lot of time and effort.

Note that the objective isn't just to make an exhaustive list of audience characteristics but to prompt you to make better decisions. For any particular decision you may find some data points don't apply. Here's the list:

Socio-economic

- Age & gender

- Income and occupation

- Places where they live (small town/big town/urban/rural) and types of neighborhood (rich/poor/aspiring/hip)

- Price vs time sensitivity

- Brands they like, wear, drive

- Social goals (to fit in/to stand out/to be first/to be life-and-soul/to be kind/to be feared/to be hip/to be traditional)

Media Consumption

- Blogs, magazines, newspapers and books they read; authors they like

- TV shows and movies they watch; directors they like. When, where and how do they watch?

- Music they listen to and bands they like. When, where and how do they listen?

Technology

- Type of cellphone they use (smartphone/basic/old/new)

- Internet speed – at home and at work

- Social networks they use (Facebook, YouTube, Twitter, LinkedIn)

If you're working for a client, you'll likely find they've grouped this data into particular customer segments and given them fancy names such as:

- Gamers

- Students

- Road warriors

- Silver surfers

- Bad Moms with Kids.

You will also have to consider the audience relationship to the client, such as:

- Current Users vs Potential Buyers

- Deciders vs Influencers

- Individuals vs Groups

- Geography (local vs national)

The strength of this segmentation is that it allows us to determine how to better deliver the experience. But it doesn't really provide guidance on what content to provide to entertain them.

5.3   ENGAGEMENT

My definition of engagement is "being in the moment". It means focusing on something to the exclusion of all else and this can apply just as well to reading a book or looking at a painting as it can to clicking around a web page.

But how does a transmedia storyteller create that engagement?

There's a great presentation on SlideShare by Jackie Turnure called *The Rules of Engagement*[36]. Her five point process for audience engagement is:

- Engage – create curiosity and suspense

- Involve – create compelling characters

- Extend – direct audience within and across media

- Surprise – keep audience on the move

- Reward – make it worthwhile.

Experienced cross-platform writer Tim Wright of XPT.com[37] has this bulleted checklist for engagement. He says your story-experience should be:

- Entertaining
- Responsive
- Responsible
- Inclusive
- Playful
- Context sensitive
- Networked
- Social
- Useful

Figure 65 shows an "experience design pyramid" that highlights how to create a compelling experience. It was brought to my attention by Gene Becker[38] and I think it's a useful diagram because it acknowledges the influence of "sensation".

I believe that sensation is often either overlooked or treated with too much importance to the detriment of the other elements. Glitzy, interactive apps can give that "wow" factor but can hide a lack of transmedia storytelling or a lack of satisfying experience. In these situations, sensation is what Robert

---

[36] http://www.slideshare.net/LAMP_AFTRS/rules-of-engagement-jackie-turnure-presentation
[37] http://www.slideshare.net/moongolfer/crossplatform-writing-presentation
[38] http://www.slideshare.net/ubik/experience-design-for-mobile-augmented-reality

McKee[39] might refer to as "spectacle". In fact, speaking with Christy Dena at Storyworld 2011 she highlighted to me three principal components that contribute to a compelling experience:

- **story** - emotional engagement with characters & plot
- **spectacle** - the wow factor and aesthetics of the work
- **process** - the mechanics of clicking, moving, exploring (online and offline)

Figure 65 Experience design

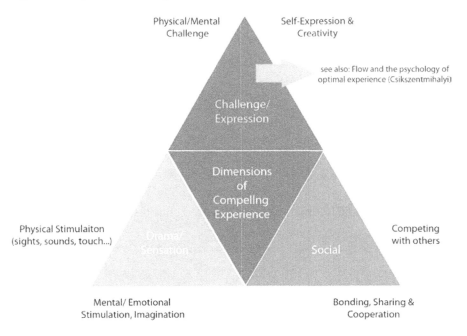

© Hull, Reid "Experience Design for Pervasive Computing"

The point of introducing engagement here is that it raises the fact that everyone is wired differently and what might engage one person might turn off another. So let's review how we might look at the audience through the lens of keeping them engaged.

5.4 PLAYER TYPES

In his excellent book *Designing Virtual Worlds*, Richard Bartle describes his analysis of MUD player types in which he asked the question "what do people want from a multi-user dungeon?" He concluded that there were four player types:

- *Achievers* – like doing this that achieve defined goals such as leveling up, gaining points etc
- *Socializers* – like hanging out with other people (either as themselves or role-playing a character)

---

[39] http://www.screenplayfest.com/ScreenplayFest/PAGES/ARTICLES/Screenwriting/interview_with_robert_mckee_writing.htm

- *Explorers* – like discovering new parts of the world
- *Killers* (also known as *Griefers*) – like to dominate and upset others!

Bartle found that each type needed another type in order to sustain their fun and engagement. If you buy his book – which I recommend you do – then you can see how these groups inter-relate to each other.

Bartle also created what he calls a Player Interest Graph – as shown in Figure 66

Figure 66 Player Interest Graph (by Richard Bartle)

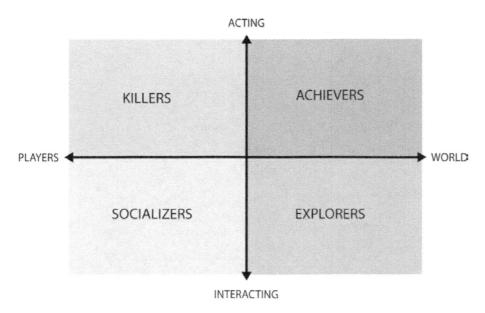

Richard Bartle, *Designing Virtual Worlds*

I was reminded of this diagram recently when I discovered Jane McGonigal's paper on the Engagement Economy[40]. In her paper you'll find a reference to Nick Yee's document on *Motivations of Play Online Games*[41] which has similar findings to Bartle's work.

Also in McGonigal's paper is a reference to Nicole Lazzaro's *Emotional Goals of Players*[42]. In Lazzaro's paper she identifies four keys to unlocking emotion in games (illustrated in Figure 67):

- *Hard Fun* - players who like the opportunities for challenge, strategy, and problem solving. Their comments focus on the game's challenge and strategic thinking and problem solving.
- *Easy Fun* - players who enjoy intrigue and curiosity. Players become immersed in games when it absorbs their complete attention, or when it takes them on an exciting adventure.

---

[40] http://www.iftf.org/node/2306
[41] http://www.nickyee.com/pubs/Yee%20-%20Motivations%20(in%20press).pdf
[42] http://xeodesign.com/whyweplaygames.html

- *Serious Fun* - players who get enjoyment from their internal experiences in reaction to the visceral, behavior, cognitive, and social properties.
- *People Fun* - players who enjoy using games as mechanisms for social experiences and enjoy the social experiences of competition, teamwork, as well as opportunity for social bonding and personal recognition that comes from playing with others.

Figure 67 Four Keys to Unlock Emotion in Games

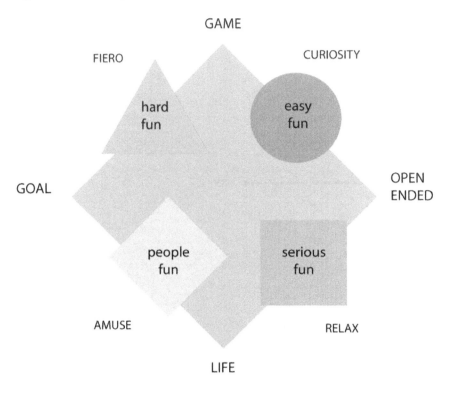

(c) Nicole Lazzaro, www.xeodesign.com

Again, it's possible to see echoes of similar findings to Bartle's work and I decided to map Yee's and Lazzaro's work to Bartle's Player Interest Graph as shown in Figure 68.

Figure 68 Goals by Audience Interest

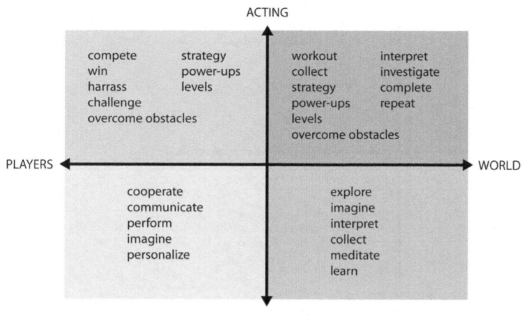

If these are the benefits being sought by audiences, then it's now possible to convert this into a content map that shows what content is most likely to appeal to particular groups of the audience. This is shown in Figure 69.

The importance of this is that we can now check our content to see if we're pulling too hard in one direction; for example, too much content aimed at *Explorers* and not enough content for *Achievers* or *Socializers*.

Always remember that I think of transmedia content as being recursive – meaning that although the ARG is shown here as fundamentally a game, in designing the ARG you would take a more granular approach and look at the specific content of the ARG and how it appeals to each player type.

To summarize then, in designing your content strategy, look to provide something for each of the four audience types and do so in a way that offers opportunity for attention, evaluation, affection, advocacy and contribution.

Figure 69 Content by Audience Type

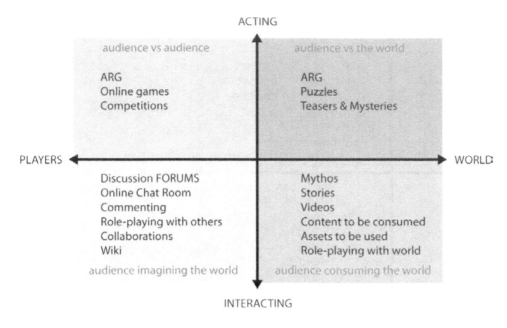

5.5 MOTIVATION

A person's motivation to engage or continue engaging over time can be thought of in terms of extrinsic motivations and intrinsic motivations. Extrinsic motivation is offering people rewards like badges, points and prizes – they are motivated by external factors – whereas intrinsic motivation is where someone takes part in an activity because it is personally rewarding to them.

The reason I avoid using terms like "gamification" is because of the negative image it has of bribing people with badges and points for doing crass or mundane things. This is extrinsic motivation. It's unfortunate to say though that it often works. The problem is that when the badges and points run out or if the prizes aren't big enough, then so does the audience participation.

In my own work, stimulating the audience to act through intrinsic motivations is the primary design criteria. This means that I attempt to design experiences in such a way that participation is reward in itself. The four primary design pillars being:

- Allow audience autonomy to explore the story in their own way
- Provide opportunities for the audience to connect with each other and with characters
- Provide opportunities for the audience to gain a sense of accomplishment
- Allow the audience to feel special or gain significance.

I'll explore this more in Section 5.5.2 but first let's look at the badges.

5.5.1 EXTRINSIC MOTIVATIONS – BADGES AND REWARDS

Although I have to admit that they work, I feel that badges and rewards can be very blunt tools for motivating people. However, there's no denying that we like receiving them. So here's my thoughts on "best practice" in using badges and rewards in transmedia storytelling.

Consider badges and rewards in the following ways. To:

- Signal what's possible, what's expected and how to get the best experience
- Incentivize good behavior
- Reward loyalty and "personal development".

5.5.1.1 SIGNALING

Transmedia experiences tend to be unfamiliar to many people and your particular project might be quite unique even to the experienced participant. Showing what badges are available for certain actions can highlight possible paths through the experience and indicate the importance of making the right choice.

This is can be seen in practice when badges are shown as locked – usually with a short cryptic or pithy description to entice and tease players to find out what they might do to earn it. For example "find the secret of the old man" or "jump four cars and spin on dismount".

Badges, perhaps when they are available in a series and imply a progression (barista 1, barista 2 etc.) can be used like a development map – showing how someone or the character they control can improve through the experience.

5.5.1.2 INCENTIVIZING & REWARDING

People like receiving badges because they provide feedback about their progress and shows to the world their competence at the game and gives them a recognition for their work. This sounds straightforward enough but some people are driven to achieve rewards so much that they will do almost anything to get them. This means that you should choose wisely when you decide what to reward as ill thought out badges and points can lead to overly aggressive or spammy player behaviors.

For example, if you plan to reward players for activity on social media it might be necessary to limit the points received to once per day so that someone doesn't keep posting banal comments or images purely for the sake of gaming the points system.

As I've advocated in other parts of this document, if your experience is to be discovered and advocated for you will need to include some kind of social component and this means players talking or working with other players. What we want is for everyone to play nicely together and get along – the more friendly and sociable the experience so that longer the experience is likely to last.

In our work with Alison Norrington[43] and Harlequin Mills and Boon for Alison's *The Chatsfield*[44] experience, we developed a range of badges to encourage behaviors most likely to sustain the storyworld. Figure 70 shows how we approached the task by considering the individual behaviors and community behaviors:

- **Good community behavior** - any activity that promotes and strengthens the Chatsfield community

- **Good individual behavior** - individual activity that will enhance and improve the experience of each person in the Chatsfield world (both in world and out of world).

Figure 70 Encouraging good behavior and a good time

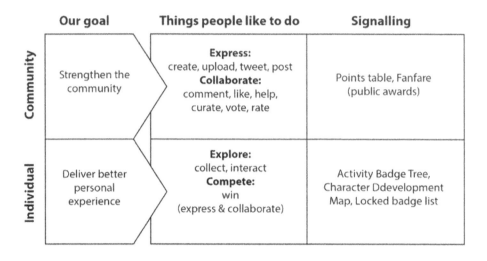

The badges we developed were in three categories:

Hotel badges	these reward loyalty and community contribution
Character badges	these reward community contribution and multi-platform engagement
Game badges	these reward quest completion, activity, achievement and excellence.

Figure 71 shows the full badge table indicating when the badge would be awarded and what behavior it was rewarding.

---

[43] https://twitter.com/storycentral
[44] http://www.conducttr.com/success-stories/the-chatsfield/

Note that rewards are in two categories:

- Loyalty – long term, frequency and volume of activity
- Personal development – hardwork, excellence, multi-platform engagement, quest completion, social standing and community contribution.

Figure 71 Summary of Badges for The Chatsfield

Category	Badge Name	Behaviour that's rewarded	How is it achieved	Bonus Points
Hotel - rewards loyalty and community contribution				
	Guest in Residence	long-term engagement	Active on at least one channel at least once a week for 12 weeks	200
	Best Friend Forever	long-term engagement	Active on any platform 3 days a week for 10 weeks	250
	Insomniac	frequency of engagement	Active on at least one channel 5 nights consecutively (after 8pm)	50
	Frequent flyer	frequency of engagement	Active on at least one channel every day for 5 continuos days	50
	Super Social Guest	loyalty and volume of activity	10 interactions in each of the Hotel platforms (twitter, Facebook and Theatrics)	150
	XOXO Gossip girl	volume of activity	10 Theatrics comments or posts	100
	Twitterholic	volume of activity	10 Tweets or re-tweets	100
	Socializer	volume of activity	10 Facebook posts or comments	100
	Lounge Lizard	volume of activity (outstanding)	30 Theatrics comments or posts	200
	Twitter Evangelist	volume of activity (outstanding)	30 Tweets or re-tweets	200
	Facebook Ambassador	volume of activity (outstanding)	30 Facebook posts or comments	200
Character - reward community contribution and multi-platform engagement				
	Intrigued Caller	personal behaviour	Call every character with a phone	50
	Early Riser	personal behaviour	5 interactions with any character before 8am	50
	Late night cruiser	personal behaviour	5 interactions with any character after 8pm	50
	Ally's Ally	character interaction	5 interactions with Ally	50
	Jessie's buddy	character interaction	5 interactions with Jessie	50
	Adam's confidant	character interaction	5 interactions with Adam	50
	Cocktail lover	character interaction	3 emails to Daniel's Bar	50
	Jessie's BFF	volume of interaction and initiative	having called Jessie to both numbers, SMS mobile, and 5 interactions in total (Facebook, Twitter or email)	150
Game - reward quest completion, activity, achievement and excellence.				
	Jessie's helper		Start the game	40
	Digging and digging		SMS character Sara Ortiz to find our about Daniel's life	40
	Curious and helpful!		Email Jessie: Daniel is the CEO at Northcom Security	50
	Meticulous and committed!		Email Jessie: Daniel's father was killed in car accident	50
	Getting the dirt on Dan		Email Ally: Daniel is a secret millionaire	40
	How clever		Solving what the 1612 means (Asking detective)	40
	Detective on the go		Discover Javier's alibi. He's not guilty.	50
	Inquisitive!		Discover Arnaldo committed the robbery but didn't drive	50
	Sherlock		Discover Francisco was on a flight the day of the crime	50
	Super Agent		Completion of the game: Find out Matthias was the responsible.	100

Figure 72 Rewards design for The Chatsfield

	INCENTIVIZE			REWARD								
				Personal development						Loyalty		
Goal	Actions	Signalling		Community Contribution	Social standing (significance)	quest completion	multi-platform engagement	Hardwork (difficulty) of task	Excellence (peak performance)	long-term engagement	frequency of engagement	volume of engagement (amount of activity)
Good community behavior												
Signal that this behavior strengthens the community	Expression: create, upload, tweet, post; Collaborate: comment, like, help, curate, vote, rate	Points table, public badge awards (fanfare)		Badges for creativity, activity, moderation	Fanfare badges.					"Elder" badge	"Regular" badge	"Leader" badge
Good individual behavior												
Signal that this behavior will lead to a better experience (in world and out of world)	Explore: collect, interact; Compete: win	Activity Badge Tree; Character Development Map; Locked badge list				Completion badges.	Activity badges.	Achievement badge. Scarce and awarded for complex or sustained activity	Top score badge. Awarded if certain % of max possible points achieved			
BADGES										Lifetime Achievement badges. Awarded after "time served"	Surprise Badges. Badge with time-limited availability	Tier Badges. Awarded a various point thresholds
OTHER REWARDS										Weekly and/or monthly deals.	Daily deals, last minute, spot prizes	Loyalty rewards.

5.5.2   INTRINSIC MOTIVATIONS

To achieve engagement through intrinsic motivation we must design experiences that satisfy core human needs. These needs are:

- Significance (special, important, unique)
- Certainty (comfort & control)
- Variety (surprise)
- Connection (love)
- Growth (learning, mastery)
- Contribution (giving back).

In their book *Glued to Games*[45], Rigby and Ryan use self-determination theory as the basis for their "Player Experience of Needs Satisfaction (PENS)" model which seeks to understand player engagement with computer games. They identify three innate psychological needs as the basis for self-motivation:

- Competency - to be in control and seek mastery
- Autonomy - to be free to act
- Relatedness - to feel connected to others.

Let's look at what the PENs model means for us as transmedia storytellers.

5.5.2.1   *COMPETENCE*

We often think that audiences don't want to bring together multiple pieces of information because the effort is perceived as too much work for insufficient reward. This leads some to the conclusion that either "ARGS require too great a level of participation" or "it's better to bring everything together" into a single hub - for example, create a mobile or tablet app that looks like an ARG but removes the effort of the scavenger hunt.

Working with PENs leads me to believe that multi-platform scavenger hunts often lead to a feeling of incompetence because the clues and cues may not be obvious: It's not clear what the audience is supposed to accomplish and there's no feedback in the form of a reward for discovering new information.

In my work, we developed the *Communicator*[46], *a* web-app that allows a hybrid experience of distributed and centralized content and the ability to reward individual players with badges, points, exclusive content and such like.

The puzzle-heavy nature of many ARGs is a big turn off for me personally because while I enjoy spatial puzzles I don't like most other puzzles - almost anything with words, numbers, code-breaking etc. And I

---

[45] http://www.amazon.com/Glued-Games-Spellbound-Directions-ebook/dp/B004NYAH66/ref=tmm_kin_title_0?ie=UTF8&qid=1352200740&sr=8-1
[46] http://www.conducttr.com/training/be-inspired/conducttr-communicator/

have to admit that the enjoyment or lack of is related to my incompetence at being able to solve them!

Rigby and Ryan's studies show a high correlation among adventure/RPG gamers between feelings of immersion and competence. **That is, if you don't want to break the illusion, allow players to feel competent.** They state that "sustained enjoyment is a function of continued success".

ARG designs particularly and transmedia stories in general might improve by:

- starting with simple challenges that actually challenge very little but communicate to the audience that "they're doing it right". These simple challenges not only offer a low-barrier to participation (a gateway activity) but can also give an early feeling of competence. Many console games work this way - for example the start of *Far Cry 3* awards the player with a "first blood" achievement for more or less just following a dot on the screen

- provide easy and hard paths to the same solution. Often in ARGs there is only the hard path with the easy path being to go to Unfiction and see the results of someone else's efforts. While this allows the "lazy" player like myself to progress it removes the satisfaction of growing competence. While I'm "cheating" I remain incompetent and it does nothing for my self-esteem and hence I'm less motivated to stick with the experience as it unfolds

- allow for "mastery in action" - tell the audience that there's a lot riding on their next move; there's a lot at stake - but actually make the challenge commensurate with their competence. Authors can do this with our Conducttr platform by sending personalized challenges based on how a player has performed up to this point. The aggregate of each personal performance could affect the community game. That is, I might get an easy challenge and someone else a hard challenge but both need to be completed for everyone to progress

- providing feedback on progress - awarding experience points, showing % progress and giving achievements and badges.

5.5.2.2 AUTONOMY

Rigby & Ryan state that fun equals "autonomy of need satisfaction". That is, freedom to choose between increasing competence or increasing relatedness.

This freedom is similar to what is usually referred to as player agency - how free is the player to act and how meaningful are the choices available. PENs states that forced choices or Hobson's choice doesn't count - there needs to be real alternative consequences for the choices. Hence a choice of "solve the puzzle" or "don't solve the puzzle" isn't a choice at all. In transmedia storytelling while players might be free to explore different websites or physical spaces at their own choosing, how often are there consequences of not doing these things? Or the choices and consequences made known?

Particularly important for repeat play and stickiness, according to Rigby & Ryan are:

- don't imply a choice if there isn't one
- choices should increase as the game progresses.

Increasing choice will affect pacing (Section 6.4) so take this into consideration too.

5.5.2.3   RELATEDNESS

Many ARG players feel that the communities built around a game is one of the most compelling aspects of ARGs. And transmedia experiences ought to find ways to allow audiences to build a range of relationships - with friends, with strangers, with team mates and so on.

The PENs model sees relatedness as the desire to be connected to others in an authentic and supportive way. This need not only mean connected to other players but also to in-game characters.

The diagram in Figure 73 shows how good storyworlds meet the needs of fans either directly or indirectly by allowing fans to connect with each other. These relationships need to be supported by the experience.

Figure 73 Great storyworlds satisfy human needs

5.6 FOGG'S BEHAVOUR MODEL

Dr BJ Fogg from Stanford University's Persuasive Technology Lab has created the Fogg Behavior Model[47] (FBM) to identify what stops and what encourages an audience to take certain actions. He identifies three core elements that must occur at the same time if the audience is to do what we'd like it to. These elements are:

Motivation   Fogg identifies three core motivators: sensation (pleasure or pain), anticipation (hope or fear) and social cohesion (acceptance or rejection).

Ability   audiences must have the competency to act in the way you'd like. This means you can make the activity easy to do (i.e. aim for simplicity) or you have to train/prepare them. Ability relates to the audience's resources rather than only, say, practical skills. For example, if a video takes 3 mins to watch but the viewer only has 30 seconds then the behavior can't occur because he lacks the ability to complete it.

Triggers   a trigger in Fogg's model is some form of call to action like an incoming email, an alarm or a large button on a webpage. He identifies three types of triggers, the choice of which depends on the audience's motivation and ability. A facilitator trigger is used for high motivation and low ability, a signal is used for high ability and high motivation and a spark for high ability and low motivation.

Fogg's advice is to plot behavior paths that create "a chain of desired behaviors" starting with simple tasks where motivation is highest and move on to tasks that require higher ability.

5.7 MEASURING ENGAGEMENT

In 2006, Ross Mayfield stated in his blog:

"The vast majority of users will not have a high level of engagement with a given group, and most tend to be free riders upon community value. But patterns have emerged where low threshold participation amounts to collective intelligence and high engagement provides a different form of collaborative intelligence".

He coined the term "The Power Law of Participation[48]" which is shown in his diagram below (Figure 74).

---

[47] http://www.behaviormodel.org/
[48] http://ross.typepad.com/blog/2006/04/power_law_of_pa.html

Figure 74 Power Law of Participation

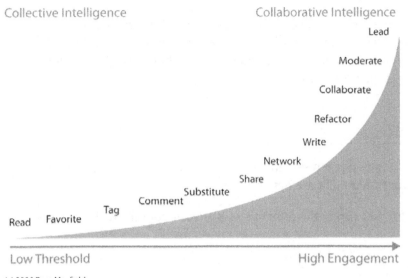

(c) 2006 Ross Mayfield

This participation curve can also be applied to transmedia worlds and will be evident to those who've run an ARG. Figure 75 shows the participation law at work in Mike Dicks[49] diagram "Rules of Engagement".

Figure 75 Audience Participation with Content

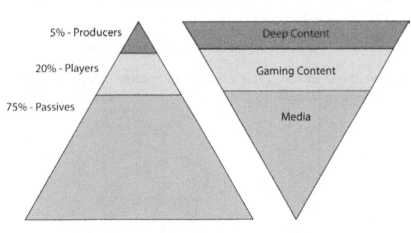

(c) Mike Dicks at BleedinEdge

What this means is that if there's less effort involved in participating in the storyworld (for example watching a video vs remixing a video) then more of the audience are likely to do it but you can't say that

---

[49] http://www.bleedinedge.co.uk/

they're as engaged with world as those who are expending more effort. More effort on behalf of the audience implies that they must be more engaged, right?   Well, yes and no.

It depends on how the individual audience member derives his or her pleasure from the world. Not everyone wants to or feels able to remix videos or contribute user-generated content yet nevertheless may be a strong advocate for the world – telling friends, family and strangers that they really ought to check out the content. Surely that's an engaged audience too?

5.8   MEASURING ENGAGEMENT

There are two ways to think about measuring engagement: in a generic way as could be applied to any content or specifically as it relates to your transmedia project.

I'll start first with Forrester's approach for measuring the effectiveness of your content which can be applied without any story framework.

5.8.1   EFFECTIVENESS OF CONTENT

Forrester Research identifies four measures for engagement with media content[50]: involvement, interaction, intimacy and influence. Developing this for our purposes of understanding engagement with a transmedia world, we should measure not only the audience's interaction and contribution but also their affection and affinity towards the world – that is, *what they say* and *how they feel* about it.

Taking this approach, a Facebook "Like", while taking such little time and effort, ranks pretty well on the engagement scale. It's more than *just any* click. It's a show of affection.

But to get that "Like" or to get a "Share", you need to provide the mechanism and the content.

Figure 76 shows the three stages of engagement – Discovery, Experience & Exploration – that inform your content choices across my five levels of increasing engagement:

- Attention
- Evaluation
- Affection
- Advocacy
- Contribution.

---

[50] http://www.dynamiclogic.com/na/research/whitepapers/docs/Forrester_March2009.pdf

Figure 76 Measuring Engagement

Stages of Engagement	Discovery		Experience	Exploration	
Level of Engagement	Attention	Evaluation	Affection	Advocacy	Contribution
Content Type	Teaser	Trailer	Target	Participation	Collaboration
Goal for your content	**Find me.** Fan comes to site and consumes low-involvement free "teaser content"	**Try me.** Fan increases engagement and consumes free "trailer content"	**Love me.** Fan spends money and decides that what I offer delivers on the promise, is entertaining and is worthwhile.	**Talk about me.** Fan tells friends.	**Be me.** Fan creates new content
How	Be relevant	Be credible	Be exceptional	Be spreadable	Be open
Measurement	views, hits, time spent per view, number for content viewed (per channel & content (e.g. emails, blogs, videos, Twitter etc.)	clicks, downloads, trials, registrations	purchases, ratings, reviews, comments, blog posts, Twitter follows, Facebook Likes, joins community	repeat purchases, subscriptions, memberships, Online: reTweets, forwards, embeds, satisfaction polls & questionnaires Offline: focus groups, surveys	Uploads, remixes, stories written, collaborations, number of fan moderators for forum, events held, other UGC

5.8.2 MEASURING TRANSMEDIA EXPERIENCES – THE TOGGLE SWITCH MODEL

During 2014 I worked on the issue of measuring engagement with transmedia experiences with Eefje Op den Buysch, Head of the Fontys Transmedia Storytelling Lab and Hille van der Kaa, professor of the professorship of Media, Interaction and Narration at Fontys School of Applied Science. What we wanted was a model that gave actionable insights to the transmedia storyteller – something that would create a heat map of what parts of the experience are working well and which parts needed improvement.

The result was Op den Buysch and van der Kaa's "Toggle Switch" model[51].

The model takes as its foundation the following understanding:

- a story-experience can be divided into scenes
- scenes can be grouped into two types: plot advancement and worldbuilding
- scenes are made up of smaller units of interactive drama called beats.

Figure 77 Foundations of a transmedia experience

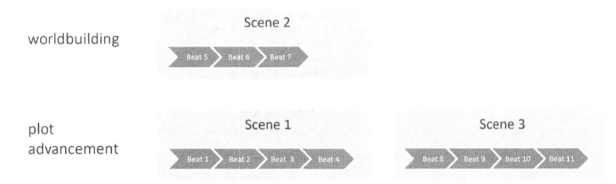

A plot advancement scene is one that takes the audience closer to the climax or resolution of the story-experience whereas worldbuilding scenes don't necessarily advance the plot but they do make a richer experience and with careful design the story more intricate. This structure is closely related to kernels and satellites as explained in Section 6.1.5.5

With this structure then, it's possible to see that we might look at how audiences navigate their way through the experience – are they very goal oriented or do they like to linger and hang out in the world exploring?

Figure 78 shows a snap shot of data taken from a Conducttr educational project. Each column represents a chapter in the experience with Ch0 being the first and Ch4 being the resolution. The numbers represent students interacting with the experience at that time – so there are 42 exploring the worldbuilding scenes of Chapter 2 and 94 trying to complete the experience in Chapter 3. You can see that this bunch of students are considerably more goal-focused (plot advancement) than interested in the worldbuilding.

---

[51] http://www.slideshare.net/eefjeopdenbuysch/transmedia-metrics-model

Figure 78 Early measurements of worldbuilding vs plot advancement

	Ch0	Ch1	Ch2	Ch3	Ch4
Worldbuilding	2	18	42	1	0
Plot Advancement	0	182	511	94	21
sum	2	200	553	95	21
WB as % Interactions	100%	9%	8%	1%	0%

The Toggle Switch model then looks at three important aspects of the experience:

- The storyworld
- The audience experience of the storyworld over time
- The individual audience member's behavior in comparison to others

With these three dimensions and the structure of Figure 77 we can track each audience member's progress through the world – each point of interaction represented by a switch that starts in the off position and is toggled on as an audience member interacts.

5.8.3 TYPICAL EXPERIENCE METRICS

To complete this chapter I'd like to finish with some charts of typical metrics you might wish to collect or present to see how your experience is performing. While not specifically indicative of engagement there are many data you might wish to collect to examine how your experience is performing.

Typical metrics will be number and timing of registrations by hour of day and day of week. A "registration" indicates when someone first becomes known to the experience (i.e. not necessarily via a formal sign-up form). Other metrics could be popularity of certain characters and popularity of channels of communication.

Figure 79 Snapshot of activity by channel

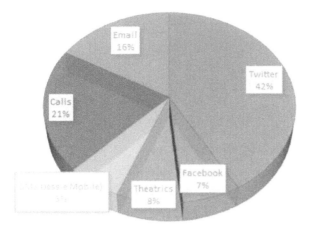

Figure 80 shows a spread of how the audience is distributed between not engaged to super engaged as measured by how many times they interacted with an experience. The chart shows that 12 people interacted only once whereas 3 people interacted 21 times.

Figure 80 Distribution of interactions

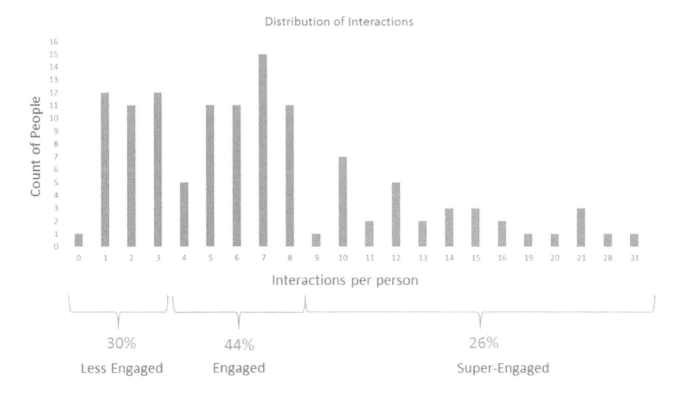

Figure 81 Last night's twitter commands

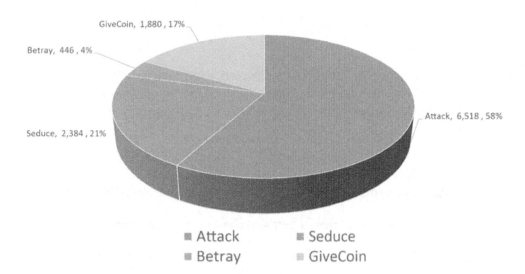

GiveCoin, 1,880 , 17%

Betray, 446 , 4%

Attack, 6,518 , 58%

Seduce, 2,384 , 21%

■ Attack   ■ Seduce
■ Betray   ■ GiveCoin

Figure 82 Registrations by group

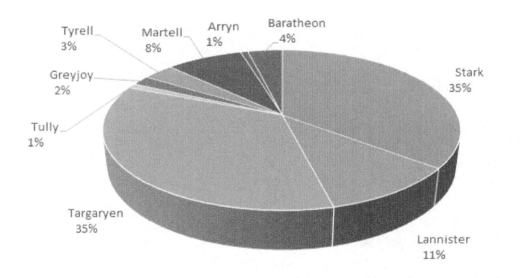

Tyrell
3%

Martell
8%

Arryn
1%

Baratheon
4%

Greyjoy
2%

Stark
35%

Tully
1%

Targaryen
35%

Lannister
11%

6   WRITING INTERACTIVE TRANSMEDIA NARRATIVES

In my line of work I've had to think very thoroughly about how people write interactive transmedia narratives and how audiences play them. And beyond the writing, how the experiences are managed and measured. Consequently I developed the four-layer model shown in Figure 83 to represent any participatory transmedia experience.

The four layers are:

Experience layer	describes the moments created and the audience' emotional journey
Narrative layer	describes the story in terms of plot and character development
Presentation layer	describes the platform, channels and media used to deliver the layers above
Interactive layer	describes the mechanics, the events and logic that deliver the experience

Figure 83 Four-layer model of interactive storytelling

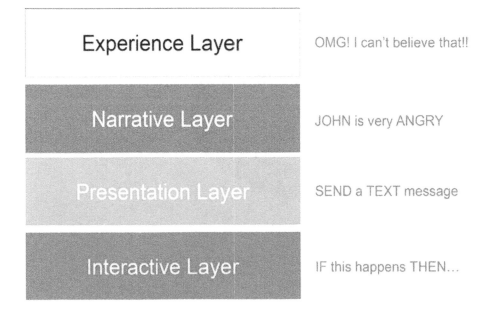

The model is useful because it highlights that:

- any given story (the narrative layer) can be delivered in a multitude of ways (presentation layer and interactive layer) – depending on audience, budget or other factors
- different documentation will be required to describe what's happening at the different layers and indeed different people may work on different layers – such as an interactive designer working at the interaction layer or graphic designer at the presentation layer.

The model also highlights the limitations of using traditional programming to code the interactive experience because while, say, a programming language like C, PHP, BASIC or whatever are efficient at doing what they do, it's impossible to see how a command like "crowd = crowd+5" relates to the story or the experience. The code is just code. Even if I write it in pseudo code such as "IF a YouTube video's views exceed 10,000 THEN send text messages to everyone" I still don't know what this means for the story or the audience experience.

So what's needed is a higher-level view of how the interactive logic relates to the other layers in the story-experience stack.

What we developed in Conducttr was our "beat sheet" – a table-like representation of the four-layer model that allows writers and interactive designers and developers to sing from the same hymn sheet: storytellers and experience designers can see their story and how it is reveled with the interaction. But more on this later. First, let's see how we can get started.

6.1 GETTING STARTED

Now, at first glance, writing for audience participation and personalization can seem very daunting but the basic steps are quite straightforward. Either:

- think of a story and then the mechanism for how it will be told
  or
- think of an experience and then a story that will hold it together.

We have to acknowledge that the story and the experience of the story work hand-in-hand – we are iteratively bending the story to meet the experience or creating an experience to deliver the story.

When developing a commercial project, certain audience actions or story points are likely to be pre-determined or mandatory (such as entering a retail outlet, say). I call these "anchors" - they are constraints or goals: things in the story or the experience that must happen. For example, a character dies or the town floods; or the audience must check in at a store or the audience must tweet a code. With skill and creativity the story-experience evolves to hit these anchors at the right time.

Figure 84 illustrates this story-experience development in the context of a three-act dramatic structure and a typical rising tension and eventual falloff at the resolution.

Figure 84 Story-experience development process

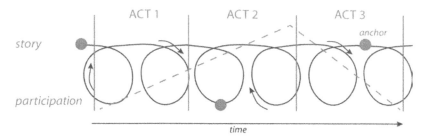

To create an interactive transmedia story, then, these are the steps to follow:

1. Write a synopsis for both the story and the audience participation
2. Break the story-experience into acts, scenes and beats
3. Create appropriate diagrams to document the experience
4. Implement technology & create the content

Note that we're working at the story-experience level now, not the project level. Figure 85 shows the project-level steps to developing a transmedia project around a potential movie re-imagining of The Mask of the Red Death. What I'm describing in this section is the individual story-experience such as would be shown in the illustration as "Psychophol Experience", say.

Figure 85 Project-level workflow for The Mask of the Red Death

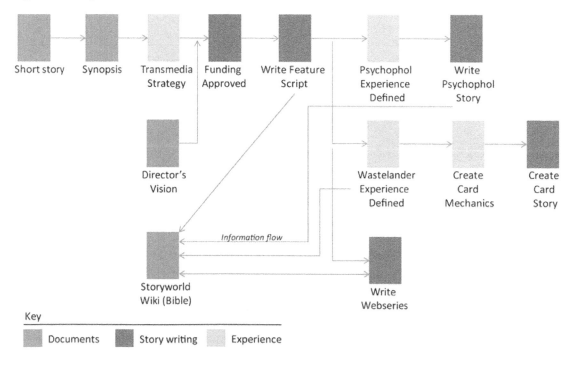

6.1.1 THE BLANK PAGE

Create a table in your word processor that has two columns. Now label one column Story and the other Experience. As the inspiration takes you, write the story and then the experience or vice versa.

Figure 86 presents the beginnings of a transmedia story. This part of the story is set in a real physical location – a bar – and ends with the audience needing to make a decision about whether to call the cops or side with the murderer. The story column is the "narrative layer" and the experience column is the "experience layer".   You can see that the "presentation layer" can creep into the experience layer because I've chosen to mention how the experience is delivered – by live action, by napkin, by phone call etc. I've used **bold** to indicate the "wow" moments for the audience: when they hear about the murder, when they realize the murderer is in the bar with them and then when they have to make a decision.

Figure 86 Example story – Jed & Sally

Story	Experience/ Participation
Jed serves drinks in a Soho wine bar. He listens to everyone's stories, he's a nice guy. He's engaged to be married.	Live action: Audience hovers by the bar listening to the stories that customers tell to Jed
A customer writes his number on a napkin and urges Jed to call him. He has something to tell him that can't be discussed in public... he leaves. Jed turns the napkin around and pushes it away... he too leaves the bar.	Physical: napkin with phone number.
Audience learns that SALLY is the murder.	Phone call: Audience calls the number and hears a recording of the customer discussing **a murder**.
A detective enters the bar and says he's looking for Jed. Anyone who knows anything should call his number – he leaves a stack of business cards	Live action: Detective and Sally alternately enter the bar and try to win over the audience. **It's her!** Physical: business cards
A woman enters the bar and asks customers for Jed. Anyone who offers to help is given her card... she is SALLY.	**DECISION**: call detective or call Sally?

Now we have a story and experience that seem to be working together we will need to break this into scenes. There's no rule about how long or short a scene should be but they will be the primary and most convenient way for you to organize your experience.

Scenes in theatre and movie scripts are based around location because this is what best relates to the production process. But with transmedia storytelling, let the narrative be the deciding factor and try to focus **on what the audience learns or discovers** because this is the source of your wow moments and cliff-hangers.

Here's what your scenes should do:

- Have goal or purpose
- Develop the drama:
    - audience discovers something new
    - audience decision or decisions moves story forward
    - brings the story or game to a conclusion

The goal is to make your scenes significant in terms of story revelations and development. When naming a scene, try to use titles that reveal the narrative – remember that you're working at the narrative layer in the model – rather than describe the presentation or interaction. For example, rather than names like "internal pub" or "makes phone call" use names like "Discovers girlfriend is a murderer" or "Audience must decide to tell police or help protagonist". We can then look at the scenes and get a bird's eye view of the narrative.

Figure 87 shows how the story-experience in Figure 86 might be broken into scenes and charted to show how the scenes are connected. The information on the arrows connecting the scenes tells us what the audience needs to do or the information it needs to progress from one scene to the next.

Figure 87 Example Scene Chart – Jed & Sally

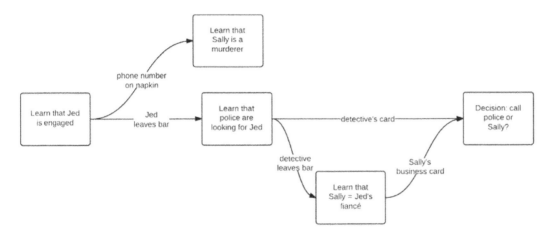

Figure 88 shows a more complex scene chart for a murder mystery in Lowlifes.

Figure 88 Scene chart for Lowlifes murder mystery

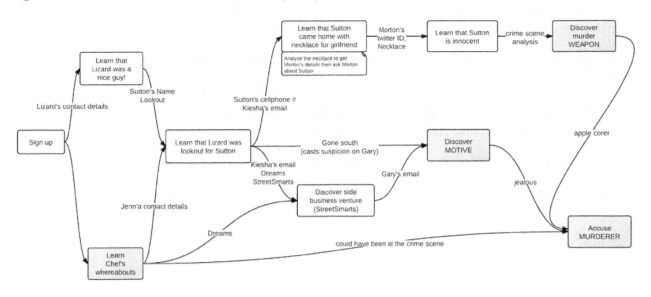

Note that the scene chart shows how the story fulfils itself and not how the audience experiences the story. For example, in the Lowlifes example above, in order to accuse the murderer the audience needs to know that the chef was jealous, that he could have been at the crime scene and that the murder weapon was an apple corer. The chart doesn't show us how the audience will accuse the chef or how it discovered the murder weapon etc.

When working with Conducttr there are also "non-narrative scenes" which might work in the background to handle game mechanics and metrics. Effectively these are subroutines or logic functions driven by events in the narrative scenes.

The next step, then, is to consider how the audience moves through a scene and from scene to scene. This is the role of the beat.

6.1.2   THE BEAT SHEET

In storytelling, a *beat* represents a development of the drama – it's a smaller dramatic unit inside a scene. This is still true with interactive storytelling but through the beat we start to connect the narrative layer to the interactive layer and presentation layer.

In a theatre or movie script, time is ultimately what advances the scene. Of course it might be an actor saying a line or smashing a vase that advances the drama but their cue is taken from timing or from other actors or events which themselves are ultimately triggered by time. With interactive storytelling, we are not limited to time cues. The scene might unfold in several minutes or several months depending on the cues or events we script.

For example, you might say "Michael will reveal his faith in a video to be published on Monday at 6pm":

we have the story "Michael reveals his faith", the presentation "video" and the event "Monday at 6pm". So the event that triggers the revelation is the time Monday 6pm. As far as the audience is concerned they are passive because Monday 6pm will happen without their involvement.

However, you could have said "Michael will reveal his faith in a video to be published when Sister Anna receives 1000 tweets with the hashtag #outhim". So now we have the same story "Michael reveals his faith" and presentation "video" but the timing is unknown – it's reliant on the audience sending 1000 tweets to Sister Anna. That might happen before Monday 6pm or never if nobody cares and doesn't tweet. The trigger event here is "1000 tweets with hashtag #outhim received by Sister Anna".

A beat, then, starts with a "trigger" – an event that moves the experience forward.

It's around this time that you might start to create a user journey (a simple example is given in Figure 89) to show the audience experience but let's stick with the beat sheet.

Figure 89 User journey for Jed & Sally

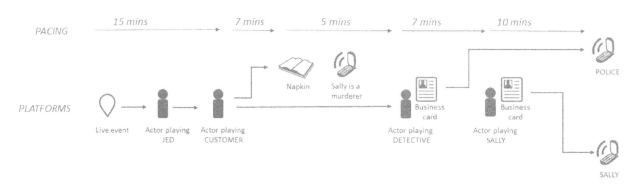

In Figure 90, we can see that the Scene "learn that Jed is engaged" contains four beats – (i) we meet Jed, (ii) we learn that he's engaged, (iii) a customer leaves a phone number and (iv) finally the audience must decide whether to call the number or not. The trigger for each beat indicates how that beat starts:

i. The audience enters the bar and that's the cue for the actor playing Jed to show how nice he is
ii. Jed follows the script and uses time and a feeling for the audience to decide when to reveal he's engaged
iii. Time passes as the customer follows the script until it comes to the moment when he reveals the number on the napkin
iv. Finally Jed and the customer have left the bar and this kicks off the final beat where the audience is left alone to decide what to do.

Figure 90 Example Beat Sheet - Jed & Sally

Scene	Beat	Trigger
Learn that Jed is engaged	Jed is a nice guy	Audience enters the bar
	Jed is engaged	Time AND audience looks to be sympathetic towards Jed
	Customer writes phone number on napkin	Time
	Audience is left alone to decide what to do next	Jed AND Customer leave the bar
Learn that Sally is a murderer	Audience calls the number	Audience makes the phone call
Learn that police are looking for Jed	Detective enters the bar	Detective waits until call is complete OR waits until it's clear they're not going to call
Learn that Sally is Jed's fiancé	Sally enters the bar	Detective leaves the bar
DECISION: call police or Sally	Audience call police	Sally leaves the bar AND audience use detective's card
	Audience call Sally	Sally leaves the bar AND audience use Sally's card

The final remaining layer to complete is the presentation layer – how the story information will be conveyed. This is shown in the updated beat sheet of Figure 91.

Figure 91 Updated example Beat Sheet with presentation layer

Scene	Beat	Trigger	Content/Presentation
Learn that Jed is engaged	Jed is a nice guy	Audience enters the bar	Script for actor
	Jed is engaged	Time AND audience looks to be sympathetic towards Jed	Script for actor
	Customer writes phone number on napkin	Time	Script for actor Hand-written Napkin
	Audience is left alone to decide what to do next	Jed AND Customer leave the bar	Hand-written Napkin
Learn that Sally is a murderer	Audience calls the number	Audience makes the phone call	Audio recording to be played if the number is called
Learn that police are looking for Jed	Detective enters the bar	Detective waits until call is complete OR waits until it's clear they're not going to call	Script for actor
Learn that Sally	Sally enters the bar	Detective leaves the bar	Script for actor

is Jed's fiancé			
DECISION: call police or Sally	Audience call police	Sally leaves the bar AND audience use detective's card	Business card Audio recording of the police
	Audience call Sally	Sally leaves the bar AND audience use Sally's card	Business card Audio recording of Sally

6.1.2.1 ACTIONS AND CONDITIONS

So far we're established that a scene describes the narrative and a beat advances the scene's narrative through one or more events. However, sometimes the "presentation" of the experience is not via content – it's via an action. For example the player wins a badge or is joined with others into a team. Then there are also, times when an event occurs and certain conditions must be met in order for an action to be taken.

For example, let's say a player is offered a simple choice: "yes" or "no". Here the trigger would be "player makes his choice" and then the content published or action taken is conditional upon the answer given – if "yes" then do x or if "no" then do y.

This Trigger-Condition-Action paradigm is the foundation of interactivity in Conducttr: storytellers tell Conducttr to listen for certain **triggers** (events) and, optionally, given certain **conditions** it will take **action** – perhaps publishing some content or doing something else:

WHEN (trigger) something happens **IF (condition)** the conditions are true **THEN (action)** do something.

The basic beat sheet in Conducttr then, looks like Figure 92.

Figure 92 Triggers-Conditions-Actions in the Beat Sheet

Scene	Beat	Trigger (WHEN)	Condition (IF)	Action (THEN)
Text field	Text field	Text field or Active trigger	Active logic or empty	Active logic and Active content

6.1.3 FIRST AND FINAL ACTIONS

While all scenes ought to be as important as each other, pay particular attention to the first and final scenes and the first and final actions of the audience.

6.1.3.1 FIRST SCENES

It's very important to immediately hook the audience. Try to get the audience to make a meaningful choice as early in the experience as possible and make it extremely simple - something with a very low barrier to entry.

Try to avoid having the audience read or explore a lot of detail before they can make the choice. One experience I can remember from 2013 had great production values but had too long an introduction - first a video... then I had to register with Facebook Connect... then I had to watch another video... by the time my choice came I'd lost interest.

A good choice is:

- meaningful
- thought-provoking
- relevant to the premise
- allows us to personalize the experience
- generates conversation
- hits as many intrinsic motivations as possible (competency, autonomy and relatedness).

Consider a simple story of boy meets girl:

- **synopsis** - *boy meets girl and boy will die. Only you can prevent it*
- **premise** - *love kills*
- **goal** - *prevent boy for getting killed*

A less than optimal first choice might be to offer the audience "who's side are you on: boy or girl?". A better choice might be: "*which do you choose: love or long life?*"

Having made a decision, we can then put the audience into two groups - the love group or the life group. We might assume that the love group is more romantically inclined and the life group is more cynical. This we can use to personalize the experience for each group so that it's more engaging.

6.1.3.2 FINAL SCENES

The final scene is of course where our story comes to an end. For the audience it must be a satisfying conclusion and leave them wishing to tell others about it.

The final action should result in the audience achieving the goal, or not, and it should result in the experience communicating the premise (e.g. *love kills*). In the simple boy-meet-girl story above, the audience must prevent the boy from being killed. We might assume that his death or the circumstances of his death will communicate the premise, but what if he lives? In this case, maybe to fulfil the premise someone else must die? In fact my solution would be to have the girl's mother kill the father. Or perhaps the mother has died a slow internal death after years of abuse in a failed marriage? This would be a rather more cynical conclusion of course and play better to the life group. So it's clear that some thought and possibly additional story content might need to be created in order to have a satisfying conclusion.

The point here is really just to highlight the importance of the final action the audience takes and make the most of it.

6.1.4   WRITING FOR ENGAGEMENT

In today's business and cultural environment there are two critical success factors:

- discovery
- advocacy.

Without discovery nobody knows your experience exists so however good your project may be it might forever sit in obscurity. Without advocacy you are forever having to "feed the funnel" manually and never able to leverage those who have discovered your experience. Further, advocacy brings recommendation and social discovery which is much stronger at eliciting trial or purchase than paid advertising.

Discovery and advocacy demand:

- a good story
- a good experience (e.g. good participation and interaction)
- a social dimension such as fan-to-fan interaction or fan-to-character interaction.

The objective is illustrated in Figure 93.

Figure 93 Intertwining story, participation and a social to create a unified experience

STORY

PARTICIPATION

SOCIAL

In writing our story-experience, then, we need to ask ourselves a number of questions:

- What social actions and conversations do I want to stimulate?
- How will I engage the audience to produce these social actions?
- What story knowledge will the audience need to engage in this way?
- Which characters/locations/things hold this knowledge and how/when will it be revealed? (i.e. the character conflicts & events plus audience interaction with the characters/locations/things)
- What's the impact on the audience when the knowledge is revealed?
- How can I empower the audience and leverage the momentum from the revelation?

Figure 94 presents these questions as a virtuous circle for engagement that binds the story to social discovery and advocacy.

Note that the importance of revealing and withholding of information in storytelling is excellently explained in Mike Jone's blog post *Secrets and Lies*[52]. Below, in Figure 95, I've tabulated the information in Mike's blog post and added my own slant by indexing everything from the perspective of knowledge. This knowledge could be personal knowledge, group knowledge or world knowledge but the point is the same: knowledge is power and the politics around that knowledge makes for great storytelling and great social action.

Figure 94 Writing for engagement

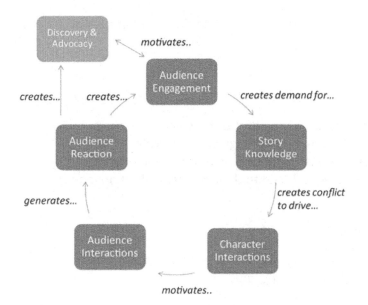

Figure 95 Knowledge is power

KNOWLEDGE	CHARACTERS				IMPACT		AUDIENCE	
Knowledge	Who Knows?	Who Doesn't Know?	Who LIES to conceal the knowledge	Who SAYS NOTHING to perpetuate the lie or keep knowledge secret	What's the DAMAGE if/when the knowledge comes out or that someone lied	What's the VALUE of the knowledge/ secret?	Does AUDIENCE know?	What's the IMPACT when audience finds out?

To get from what the knowledge means in the story to what this means in terms of audience participation, I created another table that starts with what we want the audience to do.

In Figure 96 I've listed a number of basic "social actions" - activities I want to encourage the audience to do. These actions could engage the audience with the story or could engage the audience with each other.

---

[52] http://www.mikejones.tv/journal/2011/2/17/subtext-secrets-and-lies-part-1.html

Figure 96 Audience social actions

Social Action	Required Knowledge	How is Knowledge Acquired?
Discuss...	Who was where the night of the murder	Interview witnesses & suspects
Find...	Murder weapon	Search of crime scene
Solve...	Murder's name & motive	Interviews, searches, analysis
Choose...	Confront early or wait for more evident	Analysis, discussion, gut instinct

Using the two tables above we now have a bridge between the story to be told and what the audience is required to do to have that story revealed to them.

6.1.5   PERSONALIZATION

Unique experiences create engagement and conversations: we want to share and compare our experiences with others. Personalizing an experience can mean a range of things from allowing the audience to upload a profile picture to responding with their name in an email to allowing them the freedom to choose which parts of a storyworld to explore. I tend to think of personalization in four categories:

Customization   certain details can be changed such as name, contact details, language

Historical   knows about my past choices and past actions such as did I upset a certain character, did I choose the knife over the gun

Contextual   knows about my current circumstances such as whether it's raining, whether I've been exercising, whether it's a Monday, whether it's hot in here

Interpretation   how might this message or request be interpreted by different people.

The only reason for not personalizing an experience is the cost. Personalization can add complexity and additional content so there is always a trade-off to be made about how far you go with this.

6.1.5.1   CUSTOMIZATION

Customization is relatively easy to achieve because it doesn't affect the narrative. That is, a certain email will be sent or a choice offered regardless of a person's name or preferred language. Creating this customization only needs some consideration for how this information will be gained or requested.

Technically it usually involves "smartwords" or replacement blocks of text or images based on the player's preferences.

6.1.5.2   HISTORY-BASED PERSONALIZATION

A choose-you-own-adventure story is a form of history-based personalization in that the current set of choices or circumstances depend on the decisions of the past.

It's also possible that the player's ability to act on a current event is dependent on inventory that was collected prior to this moment.

This type of personalization is the most common in games and while it shows the player that they have a good degree of autonomy, it can take a lot of work – some of which might never get seen (especially in the case of branching narratives).

A great approach to achieving this type of personalization with not so much work is to have characters adopt a different tone of voice based on how aligned the player is to the character. This doesn't require a branching narrative and has the advantage of making the experience feel personalized and that choices matter.

6.1.5.3 CONTEXTUAL

Contextualizing an experience might start by taking data from the real world – the temperature, the weather, the player's location or heartrate and so on – and then mixing this into the experience. It might be used to branch the narrative or to customize it depending on the amount of time and money available.

Figure 97 shows some example data types that could be used to make the experience seem very personal and dynamic. While incorporating this data could significantly increase the complexity of designing the experience, it can be managed by thinking in terms of kernels and satellites (see Section 6.1.5.5) – and if necessary limiting contextual personalization to satellite scenes that don't affect the core plot.

Figure 97 Data types for contextualizing an experience

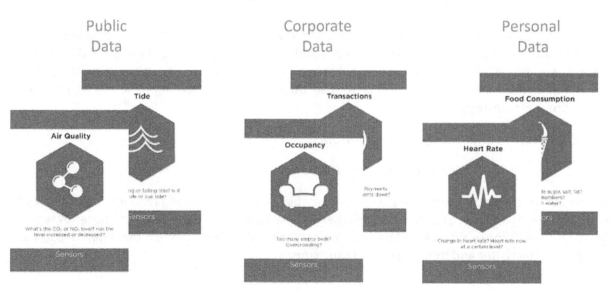

Figure 98 shows an example of how an experience might be personalized based on whether a person has been active (as measured by, say, steps recorded on a pedometer) and how frequently they visit a location (in this case a pub – which could be virtual or physical).

The first character, the pub's "Local Regular", greets the audience differently depending on the person's activity while the "Bar Tender" tailors his greeting based on the number of times the person has visited the bar. Hence the experience is personalized without affecting the core plot.

Figure 98 Contextual personalization example

Contextual Event	Local Regular		Bar Tender	
	Activity		Frequency	
	Condition 1	Condition 2	Condition 3	Condition 4
	He's not been active today	He has been active	He's never been here before	He's a regular
Man walks into a bar	"Taking it easy, huh?"	"Man, you look whacked! You've earned yourself a drink"	"Welcome to our humble watering hole. Make yourself at home"	"The wanderer returns! Great to have you back"

6.1.5.4 INTERPRETATION

I'm a strong believer that the creator should know what he wants to say with his work but allow some ambiguity to make the experience engaging.

All stories are a collaboration between the audience and the writer. Each of us brings our own unique filters and interpretations that color the writer's words and lead to a different experience. It's this ability to "speak to the audience" that sets a great storyteller apart from a mediocre one. When everything "is on the nose" and there is no room for the audience to think through the unspoken then the stories are often melodramatic or uninteresting.

For example, let's say we send a single Tweet or an SMS:

"Someone close to you does not see your aura"

Although the author speaks the words, the message is ambiguous enough for the reader to color this with his own imagination and filters: does the message mean "close" physically right now? Or "close" in terms of relationship? Does it mean that a loved one doesn't appreciate me? Does it mean that I have a psychic energy? Together the writer and the reader create the story.

6.1.5.5   *PERSONALIZATION USING KERNALS AND SATELLITES*

Espen Aarseth's work on the narrative theory of games[53] is well worth checking out as it looks at the relationship between game and story and it's where I first encountered the reference to kernels and satellites (from the book *Story and Discourse: Narrative Structure in Fiction and Film* by Seymour Chatman). From Chatman:

Kernels   Key events. "Narrative moments where the course of events is decided"

Satellites   Minor events. "do not entail any choice, but serve to flesh out the consequences and details of the kernels"

As mentioned earlier, personalization usually costs more in terms of additional design work and additional content. By thinking in terms of kernels and satellites we can increase personalization while holding down the cost by loading the satellites with contextual and historical personalization.

From any basic story, then, such as that shown in Figure 86, we can now start to improve it by adding personalization without adding significant additional complexity if we limit personalization of kernels to customization and limiting historical and contextual personalization to satellites.

If we then allow the audience to role-play in our world and tell their own stories from the foundations we give them, we see the huge potential for a personalized experience without significantly multiplying the possible story endings (which means reduced cost).

Figure 99 shows a dynamic data-driven base of world building scenes that provide a rich environment for the creator's stories (principally the kernels with satellites interfacing with the worldbuilding) and player stories.

Figure 99 Managing personalization

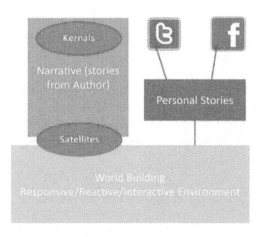

---

[53] http://vimeo.com/7097715

6.2 CHARACTER CONSIDERATIONS

Characters are the glue that engages audiences between video episodes, between TV seasons and between platforms. Characters are therefore an important part of the story but here we'll look at their role and relationship to the audience as part of the experience design.

It's important to note that our brains make no distinction between stories and real life - we perceive imagined and real events as though they were the same thing. This is why good stories are addictive - they satisfy to our core human needs. Even a connection to a fictional character is interpreted by the brain as it would a connection to a real person!

In writing a story, you might identify the following character types:

- protagonist (hero)
- antagonist (villain)
- sidekick/friend
- mentor
- rival
- skeptic.

In *gaming*, characters are used to fulfill different roles. In Jesse Schnell's excellent book *The Art of Game Design*[54], he lists these characters:

- Hero - the character who plays the game
- Mentor -the character that offers advice and useful items
- Assistant - a character who offers occasional tips
- Tutor - a character who explains how to play the game
- Final Boss - the villain the player must defeat in the last battle
- Hostage - a character to rescue.

The characters are there to support the audience through the game and increase engagement by meeting those three intrinsic needs: competency, autonomy and relatedness.

Rigby and Ryan believe that character dialogue is important to support the "player's autonomy and sense of competence" - for example in providing feedback when the player achieves something. They also say that character dialog can significantly enhance the satisfaction of a player's need for relatedness and this is best accomplished by 'positive contextual feedback'. That is, telling the player "well done! you're doing it right" or "That salesman is an idiot, you sure showed him!"

---

[54] http://artofgamedesign.com/

6.2.1 IDENTIFICATION

When we read a book or watch a movie, our engagement is based on an identification with the characters - usually the protagonist. We never confuse our own identity with that of the character - they are themselves and we are ourselves - but we empathize with the character and can imagine what it must feel like to be in those situations.

In games, Jesse Schnell says "people play games not to be themselves but to be the people they wish they could be". And there's been a lot of research on player identification with characters suggesting that players do want to play an imaginary version of themselves - perhaps someone more courageous or more attractive or maybe playing a different persona (an alter ego?).

In her research[55] into the TV show *Spooks* and its online games, Elizabeth Evans found that the audience wanted a more active role but didn't want to insert *themselves* into the storyworld - rather they wanted to manipulate the existing fictional characters. We can see this desire to manipulate characters today with Twitter where the audience might well create fake accounts for fictional characters they like (or loath). One example is the case of @bettydraper from *Mad Men* who is played on Twitter by fan Helen Klein Ross[56].

The point of mentioning this is that we must create characters that the audience can identify with and in the case of inviting them to participate, *play a role* that they can identify with which might not be themselves.

6.2.2 INTERACTING WITH CENTRAL CHARACTERS

If you're concerned about someone hijacking one of your core characters then register a Twittter account, Facebook Page and other social media accounts you believe to be important to the character (Pinterest perhaps? Instagram?). Of course this is only a small safety net - maybe a fig leaf - and there's little to stop the audience registering other similar sounding accounts.

If the central characters have their story predominantly told in a book, movie or game then you need to consider whether interaction with them on social media will interfere or clash with the author's plans.

Harry Bosch[57], for example, the long running character created by Michael Connelly has matured over almost 20 books. So which Harry Bosch should be present on Twitter? Is it the current one or the favorite one? What if he were to ever get killed off - would the Twitter account continue?   Audiences already have a privileged position in being able to jump decades in the character's life from the first book to the most recent. So it's quite ok to view the character's social media accounts as being stuck in a kind of time warp in which every day is, say, 1992.

---

[55] *Character, Audience Agency and Trans-Media Drama* by Elizabeth Evans
[56] http://mashable.com/2012/03/12/betty-draper-twitter/
[57] http://www.michaelconnelly.com/extras/series/#Bosch

Authors sometimes get hung up on "reality". But we're not trying to create reality, we're trying to create engagement and we do that by sparking people's imagination. If I saw Mickey Mouse in Times Square I'd know it was a person in a costume but I can allow myself to believe. And so it is with characters on Twitter. We're not trying to *convince* people that they're real, we're helping people *imagine* a world in which the characters are real. It's entertainment; escapism.

6.2.3   INTERACTING WITH SUPPORTING CHARACTERS

Supporting characters on social media may offer more freedom because it's more likely that there are lots of gaps in their story that's not told in the "primary" (revenue-earning?) media.

There's also another reason: it allows the audience to role-play what it might be like to be someone like the central characters. For example, bringing to life Moneypenny, Q or M from James Bond allows the audience to become a secret agent - being sent on missions and having all the conversations James Bond might have.

Using secondary characters to interact with the audience allows the audience to enter the storyworld as a companion to the central character and feel what it's like to be in their shoes without necessarily being that central character or even being themselves.

6.2.4   THE AUDIENCE'S CHARACTER

Allow the audience to play as their imaginary self rather than as who they really are. Even if they play with their real Facebook or Twitter account, allow them to put some distance between themselves and the role they're playing.

You might also consider whether the audience should participate in the first person - *playing as* a character - or third person - *controlling* a character. There's a good discussion at Kotaku[58] about first and third person perspectives around immersion and whether one is better for storytelling (3rd person) and the other better for gaming (1st person).

Here are some things you might try to communicate that the audience is adopting a role rather than playing as themselves:

- when asking the audience to play in the first person
  - offer a simple choice - "who do you want to be?"
  - allow them to select a faction and a place in the hierarchy so that they play a type
  - allow them to hide behind a username
- when asking the audience to play in the third person
  - allow some modification of the character to improve identification such as choosing character

---

[58] http://www.kotaku.com.au/2011/04/first-or-third-person-whats-your-perspective

traits or clothes or friends.

It is possible to switch between 1st and 3rd person perspectives. In the project Psychophol[59] the audience registers for a clinical trial of a fake drug (first person; probably not enough of a mask to be someone else) and then follows a story and controls a character via Twitter (third person).

6.3 IMPROVING TRANSMEDIA NARRATIVES

This section first appeared as a blog post I was inspired to write after reading the paper "Improving Computer Game Narrative Using Polti Ratios" by Richard Hall and Kirsty Baird. The document had me wonder if I could create similar equations to evaluate the strength of transmedia experiences. Hall and Baird create three equations for assessing the strength of a narrative game:

Level of Drama (LoD)= P/E
P = count of all Polti situations / E = events

Variety of Drama (VoD)= U/36
U = Unique Polti situations / max 36 available

Involvement in Drama (IiD)= U/(M+5*C)
U = Unique Polit situations /
M = main characters
C = minor characters

Here's my version for transmedia which works towards a formula for more engaging experiences by looking at the creator's considerations when creating an experience – such as number of characters, channels of communication, touchpoints on and offline, impact of audience choices on the narrative and strength of the narrative.

Confusion Factor (Cf) = (M+C) * Ac
Characters x Accounts
Accounts = number of ways to contact the characters (i.e. "channels")
Goal: keep this number low (1 character x 1 account = 1 = best chance of no confusion)

Immersion (I) = P/Cf
Count of Polti units/Confusion factor
"Immersion" = likelihood of audience getting hooked (immersed). Assumption is that a stronger story makes for better immersion in the world. Note that confusion weakens the immersion.
Goal: Higher the better

---

[59] http://www.psychophol.com

Agency[60] = (Consequences/Choices)
Consequence = (knowledge to make decision x impact of decision) x story turning points.
Consequences for character ought to be consequences for audience too and vice versa. Turning point means story takes a different direction or moves towards a different final outcome
Knowledge & impact are in range 0 to 1 where 0 = no knowledge and no impact and 1 = full knowledge and greatest impact.
Goal: Higher is better

Engagement (E) = I * A / (T1 + 5*T2)
T1=Online touchpoints
T2=Offline touchpoints. Note that the 5 multiplying factor is somewhat arbitrary but implies real world activities require more effort and therefore ought to pack a great reward for the audience.
(Immersion * Agency)/(Online touchpoints + 5*Offline touchpoints)
Goal: Higher the better

Something for further inclusion and discussion is the role of time. For example, is it better for the experience to run faster than it is slower? I think this might be true. And if it is, then experiences that need to last longer need a stronger story.

6.4 PACING

In an interactive, portmanteau-type transmedia story, the author tries to give the audience a good degree of freedom to explore and investigate at their own volition while still aiming to create a satisfying dramatic storyline. Broadly speaking, making these open world, multi-linear stories thrilling can be tricky. A central problem of these experiences, assuming that a linear version of the story would be worth reading, is pacing.

Before diving into my suggestions for pacing in transmedia storytelling, let's first look at pacing in three different media:

- **Book**: The reader is free to move through the pages at their own pace and indeed she can even skip to the end and read the conclusion if so desired. Usually though the pace of the page turning will be related to the speed of reading and engagement with the story. As the plot thickens the reader is engaged more deeply the page turning speed likely increases. The feeling of pace is that the story is moving faster, developing more quickly

---

[60] For discussion of Agency I recommend reading this paper: "Commitment to Meaning: A Reframing of Agency in Games" by Karen & Joshua Tanenbaum

- **Movie**: Assuming that the viewer is unable to fast-forward, the pace of a movie is determined by the plotting, the length of the shots (e.g. editing) and the style of the shot. For example, a music video with little to no plot development can seem fast-paced because of the fast cutting and often a moving camera. Moving the camera adds energy to the shot so even when a shot is held for many seconds, tracking will prevent the shot looking static and add pace. For character-based dramas, the shots are often longer with less camera movement: if the plot doesn't develop, if we're not engaged, then the movie will feel boring because "nothing's happening"

- **Game**: There's a great presentation on SlideShare by Shiralee Saul on game pacing[61] and a much longer discussion at Gamestura[62]. Saul lists four key determinates to game pacing:

  - movement impetus - the desire of the player to move through the level
  - threat - the feeling of danger
  - tension - the mood of the level
  - tempo - the reaction speed demanded of the player and movement mechanics.

So what can we learn from this that might be applied to transmedia storytelling? In my opinion pacing in transmedia lies in the following four dimensions:

- story
  - plotting (inc. exposition vs development)
  - mood & tension
  - threat
  - impact of decision
- ability to move forward
  - number of choices available
  - ease of decision making/problem solving
  - checkpoints/gates
- required reaction speed
  - rate of content delivery
  - speed of response demanded by Author (inc. "ticking clock" & threat)
- the platform
  - length of content (e.g. time to read or watch or play)
  - ease of interaction

I've tabulated how these factors might affect pacing in Figure 100 below. Note that no single dimension can be looked at in isolation but must be considered in relation to the others.

---

[61] http://www.slideshare.net/ShiraleeSaul/07pacing

[62] http://www.gamasutra.com/view/feature/4024/examining_game_pace_how_.php

Figure 100 Controlling pacing in transmedia storytelling

Story	Increase Pace	Decrease Pace
plotting	*faster revelations*	*more backstory*
mood & tension	*fear and dread*	*relaxed environment*
threat	*imminent danger*	*safe*
impact of decisions	*big impact*	*minimal impact*
Ability to move forward		
number of choices available	*few*	*many*
ease of decision making	*easy/simple*	*tough/difficult*
checkpoints/gates	*none*	*delay progress*
Required reaction speed		
rate of content delivery	*fast*	*slow*
speed of response demanded	*quick response*	*slow response*
The platform		
length of content	*short*	*long*
ease of interaction	*easy*	*tricky*

6.4.1   IMPACT OF STORY ON PACING

Discussing pacing in story writing could be a very long section indeed so I'll take the coward's route and defer to the books on writing that deal with this - many of which do so from the particular perspective of certain genres. In this section I'm going to focus primarily on the pacing of the experience but as Figure 101 shows pacing of the experience and development of the story need to go hand-in-hand.

Something to watch out for and avoid is trying to tell too much story while encouraging the audience to act quickly. For example, a chase game or timed experience that encourages audiences to move quickly will remove the motivation to engage with the story – because story can take time which in this case would be counter-productive. Consequently it would be necessary to design opportunities for time-outs or ability to collect story content and review later.

Figure 101 Experience vs Story

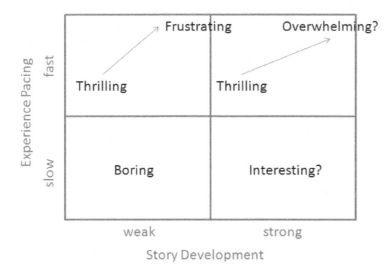

6.4.2 ABILITY TO MOVE FORWARD

If it's easy for the audience to do *something* then the feeling of pace will increase. Having the audience take action depends on the range of actions open to them (the number of choices) and the easy with which they can take an action. The "ease of decision making" depends of the impact of the choice, skill level or prior knowledge. If the audience feels fully equipped and has no dilemma then decisions are made quickly. However, get the audience to pause for thought or problem-solve then progress is slowed. I've illustrated this in Figure 102 with a table for considering how decision making and range of choices might affect pacing. Of course it's not quite that simple because the pause for thought might be for a really engaging story moment - hence possibly increasing the feeling of pace (even though progress has slowed).

Having multiple choices or actions available is a good way to have the audience control their own pace - choosing difficult paths (tough decisions to make) or easy paths (no brainers) to suit their mood. Whether all options are mandatory or all remain available after any particular choice is for the author to decide but affects the difficulty of the audience making a decision.

Figure 102 Choice and pacing

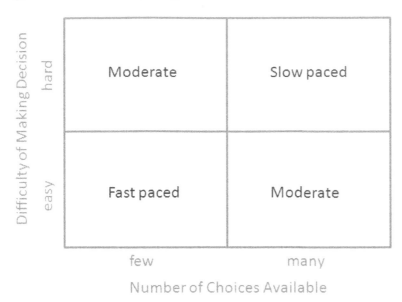

Note that one choice may lead to more choices or fewer choices. Restricting or opening up options allows for an effective pacing control but the ease of decision-making must be taken into account. A few tough choices will slow pace while a few easy choices will speed pace.

Ultimately the author might purposefully block progress with checkpoints or gates to halt advancement until, say, a certain date and time. This would be achieved by holding back the release of new content and reducing all choices.

6.4.3 REQUIRED ACTION/REACTION SPEED

One way to get the audience to react quickly is to create consequences and benefits of fast decisions. For example, an animation showing time remaining to make a decision adds tension and excitement and encourages faster decisions, a limited number of prizes, time-limited access to information or increased ranking in a leader board depending on speed of response will all provoke the audience to act quickly.

The rate of content delivery will also affect pacing - for example monthly content vs daily content. It's important that this parameter is tweaked with the content length or else the audience might feel overwhelmed and unable or unwilling to keep up (see Section 7.2.3).

6.4.4 THE PLATFORM

Finally, I believe that the platform used for the content can also communicate pace. For example, mobile SMS messages will tend to urge a faster response (increase pace) whereas, depending on length, a video or blog post might effect a slower response. Similarly, if the audience is expected to travel to a physical location to collect new instructions - this too will slow pace.

With short-form messages like Twitter and SMS, pace might be effectively communicated by the rate of delivery. For example, increasing the number of Tweets or text messages per day (per hour?) as the story reaches its conclusion would add urgency.

6.5 LOCATION-BASED STORYTELLING

Location-based storytelling has steadily been increasing in popularity and there is much to gain by applying a transmedia storytelling-based approach. Of course "location-based storytelling" encompasses a wide range of experiences – not all of which might be considered transmedia storytelling – but they certainly offer insights. First let me start with some examples.

On July 17 2015, I attended a performance of Monument[63], a site-specific theatrical performance synced to prerecorded audio played from a pre-downloaded mobile app. I might actually call this a kind of "subtle mob" – a phrase coined to infer that unlike a "flash mob", the mob attempts to blend with the public and remain unseen.

Everyone was told to meet at Charing Cross station at 8:30pm. The downloaded audio file was locked and unable to be played until it was unlocked at that specific time. What then unfolded for the next hour was effectively a play told by a handful of actors that took place in Trafalgar Square (Figure 103).

Figure 103 "Monument" by Wiretapper

---

[63] See http://www.wiretapper.co.uk/

What I loved about this was the audio design. Starting with the echoed voice of the platform announcer in Charring Cross station, the audio always sounded like it was being played in that space and not from my mobile. Several times I unhooked my headphones to check if the audio was coming from the audio track or from outside. This really did feel like a blend of fiction and reality. A particularly fun moment was when the audio synced to a regular passenger airline plane flying overhead and we listened to the activity inside the plane. To do this would have required pre-planning to make sure it coincided every day with the fly-over.

Contrast this experience, which demands I attend at a very specific time and place, with *A Hollow Body*[64] another London-based site-specific audio-based experience that can be played at any time. This is much closer to an audio walking tour except that the experience is to be played in pairs. Now, instead of actors performing, my partner and I kind of "perform" for each other.

A Hollow Body starts close to St Paul's cathedral and requires the partners to choose opposite sides of a doorway and then manually synchronize the start of the audio by pressing play together but on different buttons (left and right). We are now connected by different but matching audio files – sometimes causing us to travel together and sometimes apart –across London through a mix of less well trodden alleyways and popular public spaces.

The power of these audio-based experiences is the ability to overlay a new narrative on top of possibly familiar surroundings.

Of course not all location-based stories require pre-recorded audio. *Incitement*[65] by Splash and Ripple is, to use their words "a 2 hour theatrical street game". My friend and I took part on September 8th 2012 in Bristol, UK and the image below (Figure 104) shows the final climax in which live actors take to a make-shift stage to rally the crowd – some of whom understand what's going on and others just members of the unsuspecting public.

Incitement starts online and establishes the storyworld. At registration in Bristol at the physical, real-world start to the experience we were given armbands to indicate which faction we were fighting for and then told to visit several locations across town – avoiding apprehension by the actors who would be on the look-out for us.

---

[64] http://www.ahollowbody.com/
[65] http://www.splashandripple.com/incitement

Figure 104 Incitement by Splash and Ripple

Part of the fun of these pervasive games is the feeling of being among the public while they are unknowing. Including theatrical elements with either semi-scripted/improvised interactions or performances by actors adds to the entertainment but it's really wants going on in your imagination that makes these experiences what they are.

A final experience worth checking out is *The Roswell Experience*[66] which is documented very well in Carolyn Handler Miller's excellent book *Digital Storytelling, a creator's guide to interactive entertainment.*

So how should we approach the design of these experiences?

---

[66] http://www.conducttr.com/success-stories/the-roswell-experience/

While not hard-and-fast rules, I would say:

- if maximizing the number of people that take part is important to you, design for the experience to be location-aware, not location-dependent
- design for existing behaviors

If the story uses game mechanics to enhance the experience then:

- assume nobody will read the rules
- give rewards early and frequently

Most important of all is to know the audience and to layer the experience based on different levels of participation.

6.5.1 KNOW YOUR AUDIENCE & THE LOCATION

The first question to ask is if the experience will be an event (or series of events) or persistent. That is, will the experience run for a set period of time at a given start date & time (an event)? Or can anyone start the experience whenever they wish (persistent storyworld)?

The second question is to ask if the experience is aimed at locals or visitors. By "locals" I mean anyone local to the location... and if the location can be anywhere then all the audience is a local. By "visitors" I mean people in a different location to the one they're familiar with (e.g. not their home town).

Figure 105 shows some of the implications of these two decisions. This breakdown isn't supposed to be exhaustive but it should help you focus on exactly the type of audience you need and where you hope to find them:

- **Event for locals** - are there enough people in the catchment area willing to explore a location-based story? It's not just knowing the town or city's population - you need to be honest about who the experience appeals to and whether they have the time and inclination to take part

- **Event for visitors** - is this the best date, time and place for this story? Will there be enough visitors of the required demographic willing to take part?

- **Persistent experience for locals** - is there enough content at enough locations to accommodate this audience? Are you allowing locals to take part at wherever location they're at or do they need to travel?

- **Persistent experience for visitors** - will visitors feel they have enough time to take part? How will they know to take part?

Figure 105 Location-based story design - stage 1

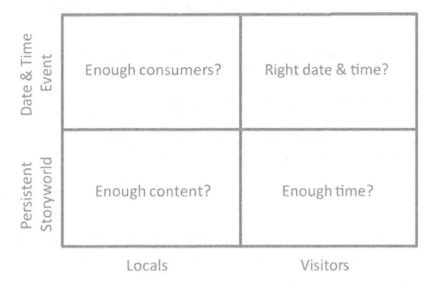

It really can't be stressed enough that you need to know at whom this experience is targeted. It's not enough to consider the basic demographics, you need to dig deeper to consider age, income, education, volume (number of people), frequency and occupancy rates (how their numbers swell and wane around the planned location during different times of the year), technographic (use of technology and services like Twitter, SMS etc).

If you're designing for a particular location, consider the traffic patterns (commuters travel by bus or car, are the roads gridlocked?), whether the location is pedestrian-friendly, climate (raining? sunny? too hot or too cold to walk about?) and of course access to 3G, wifi etc.

Considering these aspects can help you design an experience that fits existing behaviors. It might be crucial not to expect someone to do something different. If the location has two coffee shops of the same chain on either side of the same street then you know that in this town people can't be bothered to cross the road for a coffee so why will they do anything for you?

6.5.2   LAYER THE EXPERIENCE

For persistent stories, requiring someone to go to a particular location is immediately going to reduce the number of people taking part. Firstly, the location may not be convenient and secondly most people can't be bothered to try something new. The key, therefore, if it's at all possible, is to make the story location-aware rather than location-dependent. This means allowing anyone to access the story online (from the comfort and security of their home or office) and using real-world locations as added-value.   In the case of the audio-based examples given earlier this sounds completely inappropriate but you might consider starting with some online, easier-to-experience content ahead of the main event.

If a local business wants people to visit its store, find a way to represent the store online and entice people to the store with additional content, power-ups, level-ups and any number of other incentives but avoid making it mandatory. Requiring anyone to go to a specific location is likely to create a road block which could result in someone abandoning the experience.

If you think about the places you've wanted to visit because they were mentioned in a book or used in a movie, the enticement came from the lowest form of participation - reading or viewing.

For event-based experiences, make sure that you start the recruitment of players early and use online resources to capture the largest possible number of people. In this you may be expecting people to travel to a specific location at a specific date and time so make sure you make it easy by providing all the information they might need and make sure there's enough time to plan the travel.

6.5.3   PUTTING IT ALL TOGETHER

Having decided the type of experience you want to create, who it's targeted at and where it'll play you can now start to write the story and the audience participation[67]. The workflow is shown in Figure 106.

Note that the final stage is to consider how the audience will find out about the story - these are the "discovery touchpoints". It might be online and it might also be flyers at the actual location. Be very clear about discovery and the call-to-action.

If you're involving local businesses, make sure it's clear that they know they're a discovery touchpoint (you might not want to use that jargon though!). That is, have them agree to have a flyer or poster in their window, have a custom table flyer or beer mat, a point-of-sale display and importantly make sure staff are informed and encouraging people to play. Don't require passersby to go into the store to take part but add value if they do.

If you have a game-based experience:

- assume that nobody wants to read a bunch of rules before they start engaging so try to have the rules reveal themselves through the play

- make it easy to get hooked with simple casual games as well as or instead of more difficult scavenger hunts and puzzle solving

- give rewards early and frequently so that players know they're doing the right thing and are encouraged to continue

- keep everything very simple and frictionless which means low intellectual demands, physical demands, time demands and technology demands. Every time you increase one of these factors above the minimum you reduce your potential audience.

---

[67] If you're ever looking for inspiration, check out the work of Mark Shepard at http://www.andinc.org/v4/

Figure 106 Location-based storytelling - decision flowchart

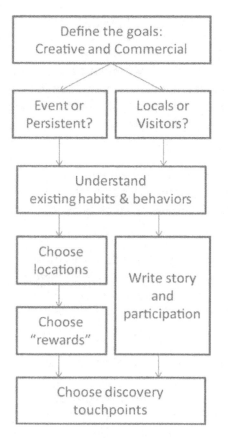

6.6 THE INTERNET OF THINGS AND OBJECTS THAT TELL STORIES

The Internet of Things (IoT) is a term used to describe the trend towards everyday objects being connected to the Internet. The usual examples are a fridge that can tell you what's inside or a car key that reports its whereabouts should you lose it.

For storytellers, intelligent objects offer a new platform that mixes the physical world with the digital.

There have been some interesting research projects. Among them Treasure Trapper[68] which asks the audience to catch virtual objects as they leave a museum on public buses and at the time of writing Lance Weiler's *Sherlock Holmes and the Internet of Things*[69] which is attempting to create globally connected crime scenes – using participatory storytelling with objects left around a crime scene to help audiences construct their own stories. Figure 108 shows my initial thoughts for how we might connect crime scenes

---

[68] http://www.chrisspeed.net/?page_id=1576
[69] http://sherlockholmes.io/

to allow physical objects in Madrid to have a virtual presence in London and elsewhere.

In my own work we've been considering how objects might tell their own stories and how they might help people connect with each other[70]. Here's a video playlist[71] of the fun we've had so far.

Quite where storytellers will take smart objects as a medium is still unknown but my thoughts are that the objects are treated as characters – with histories and secrets that are revealed through interaction (or being left idle?). Maybe the objects have goals. For example a detective's briefcase might need to be filled with evidence and it could complain if were not filled. What if a digital object were "fragile" and degraded with every scan – leaving less and less of a story over time?

Imagine then a bloody knife that knows its history (See Figure 107). At its birth it was not a murder weapon and may have been in several locations and had several owners. How much does it remember of the fateful day when its owner used it with malice? Maybe its memory is unlocked through questioning or proximity to other smart objects.

Another aspect is modelling the physical object with a virtual companion or representation. This means that every audience member has their own interpretation of the object based on any number of factors – time and place of interaction, previous interactions and so on. And in a connected world, how intelligent does the object really need to be? Can we have "dumb" connected objects where the story is held in the cloud? The likelihood is that we'll want both.

If objects are connected and people are connected to objects then that means people connected to people via the objects. This opens opportunities for collaborative play and storytelling (and of course competition). There's long been a history of people leaving messages for others – recorded on paper in geocaches to recorded digitally at a location and unlocked with GPS to recorded digitally with an object. Typically NFC has been used as the digital tag that identifies the object and hence allows someone to access its stories.

A message in a bottle is a well-known storytelling object from the past connecting people across oceans. In the digital age, how can we create the romance of a message in a bottle with the wonder of a ship in a bottle?

---

[70] http://www.conducttr.com/training/conference-2014/the-storyworld-of-things/

[71] https://www.youtube.com/watch?v=fAx--CJcAIk&list=PLbwry1jJeXZEXt5q9EkjDE4HRhtudTRo7

Figure 107 Objects that tell stories

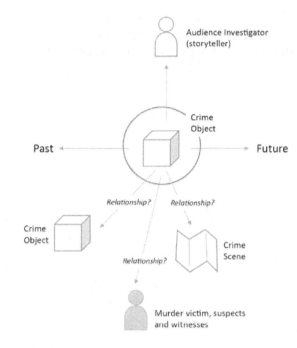

Object has its story to tell

If a knife could speak about what it knows of the crime, what would it say?
Interactive Narrative Choices:

a. *"output" HOW does object TELL it's story?*
   How does it "speak"? → haptic? Light? screen? Immediately or delayed? On this object or on another object/device?

b. *"input" WHAT unlocks the story? What are the possible parameters → time? proximity (to audience, to other objects, to locations), interaction, number of interactions, combinations of these...*

Audience generates its story

Goal: audience pieces a narrative from the storylets given by various objects. It's their imagination that "connects the dots". One person's interpretation might not be another's.
Interactive Narrative Choices:

a. *"output" HOW do others connect with someone's story? Online? In person? How do we share each other's stories?*

b. *"input" HOW to they communicate their ideas/their story? Should the audience communication be tagged into conclusions, suggestions, questions?*

Figure 108 Connected crime scenes

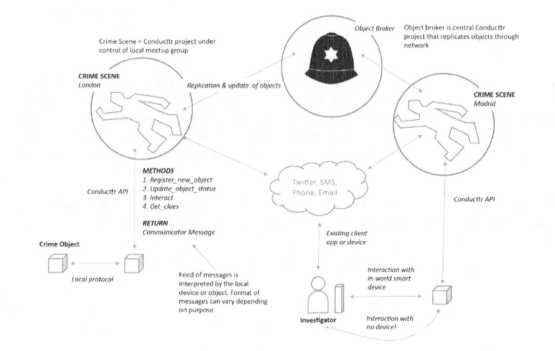

6.6.1 A FRAMEWORK FOR THINKING ABOUT OBJECTS

Figure 109 shows a framework for identifying the possibilities that objects offer. The notes in the illustration refer to a "product" and of course it could be box of cornflakes or a pair of sneakers. Whatever the object, how can we use it to bring people together? How can we have the object tell our story?

Figure 109 Socializing objects

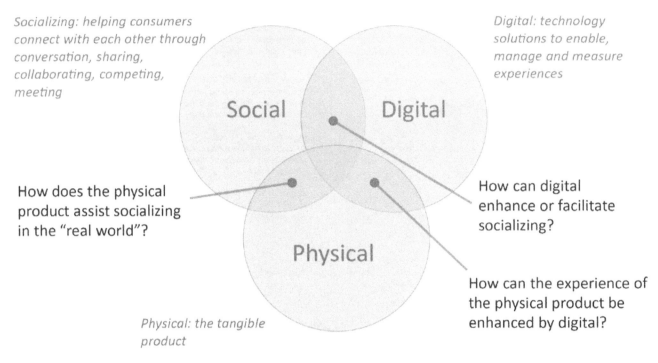

Socializing: helping consumers connect with each other through conversation, sharing, collaborating, competing, meeting

Digital: technology solutions to enable, manage and measure experiences

How does the physical product assist socializing in the "real world"?

How can digital enhance or facilitate socializing?

How can the experience of the physical product be enhanced by digital?

Physical: the tangible product

Figure 110 is a product concept I created to illustrate a point. It's a new energy drink for gamers to keep them awake through long nighttime game sessions. The packaging is designed so that it can be stacked to create interesting patterns that could be photographed and shared online. Note the multiple points where straws can be inserted – allowing packs to be held together with straws in different configurations. Hence the packaging is more than just a container for drink, it's also a construction block and social storytelling object.

How could this packaging cross over into the digital world through more than just the sharing of a photograph? Could pattern recognition be used to draw the object into a virtual world?

Figure 110 A social object as drink packaging

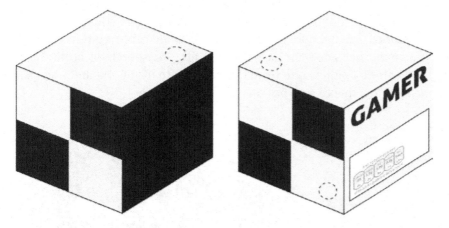

Figure 111 Telling my story with the objects you give me

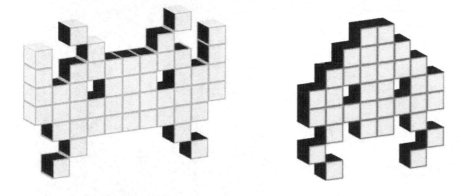

6.6.2   IN WORLD AND OUT OF WORLD

Having a storyworld blend with the real world through physical objects is a lot of fun and is often used in promotion. For example, you might see graffiti tags from a fictional world sprayed on a building wall or real people in costumes of fictional characters in a shopping mall or that bench[72] with a fictional advertisement from the world of District 9. Figure 114 shows a poster for a fictional drug intended to get people engaging online.

Of course the blending of fictional and real needn't be limited to the physical world, the "fake" TEDx video[73] for the movie Prometheus is a great blend of fiction and reality and websites for fictional people, places, companies and products is commonplace.

---

[72] http://cdn.creativeguerrillamarketing.com/wp-content/uploads/HLIC/d218f2f8dc3708bc5894ab81bf21cf72.jpg
[73] http://www.youtube.com/watch?v=0EVFrSuyA-c

Figure 112 illustrates how we might look for opportunities to spread our fiction into the real world using retail spaces, product packaging and such like. The photograph is mine from work we did for CANAL+Spain for Game of Thrones. It's one of a series of posters found in FNAC stores that changed weekly with new stories from our world of 19 Reinos. The stories explained an event in the world and reported that the reader had found money "Here lies a merchant that's been attacked by bandits. You search his body and find 5 gold coins". The reader would then enter a unique code from the poster into his phone and unlock virtual currency that could be spent on weapons, shields and potions in the MMORPG.

Figure 112 Spreading fiction into the real world

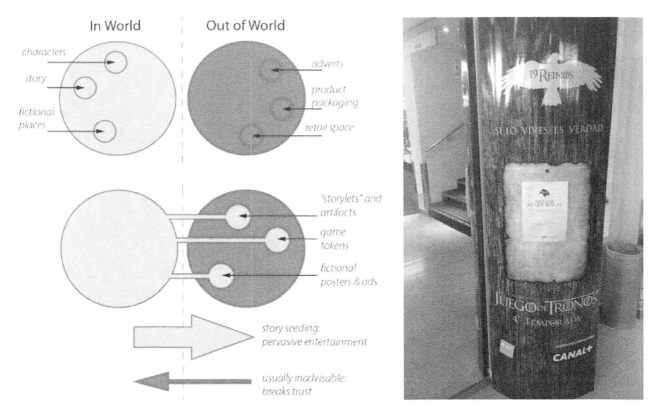

In the project FutureCoast[74] created by Ken Ekland[75] and produced by Sara Thacher[76], artifacts from the future were hidden around the (real) world and audiences invited to find them. These beautiful artefacts, known in-world as "chronofacts" were a mechanism for audience participation. Upon discovery, the finder was encouraged to decode it and listen to the voicemail from the future about how climate change[77] had

---

[74] http://futurecoast.org/

[75] http://writerguy.com/

[76] http://thachr.com/ be sure to checkout Sara's excellent blog post on "Tangible Storytelling"

[77] https://www.youtube.com/watch?v=AffkjJ-Ft64

affected this character. The finder was then encouraged to write or call to leave their own in-world message from the future.

Between February and May 2014, 42 "chronofacts" were discovered and more than 300 voicemails recorded. Figure 113 shows a lucky finder Vicky Peter in the Marshall Islands[78]. The chronofact shown in the photo decodes to the voicemail "Another Die-Off"[79] from 2025.

Figure 113 Victorina (Vicky) Peter with Chronofact #59908-22066305[80]

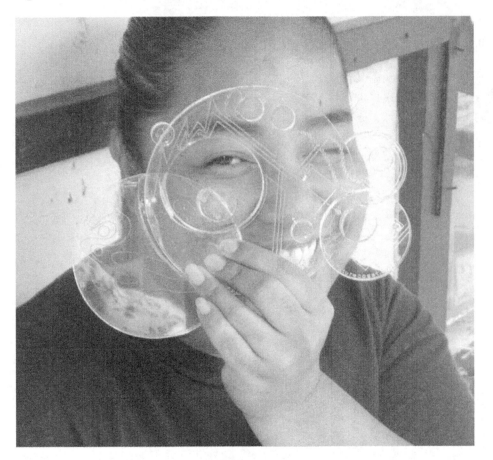

---

[78] Map link to the Marshall Islands
[79] http://futurecoast.org/voicemail/59908-22066305/
[80] Found in Majuro, Marshall Islands. Photo by Fern Raffela Leyman, College of the Marshall Islands

Figure 114 Psychophol – a real-world poster for a fictional drug[81]

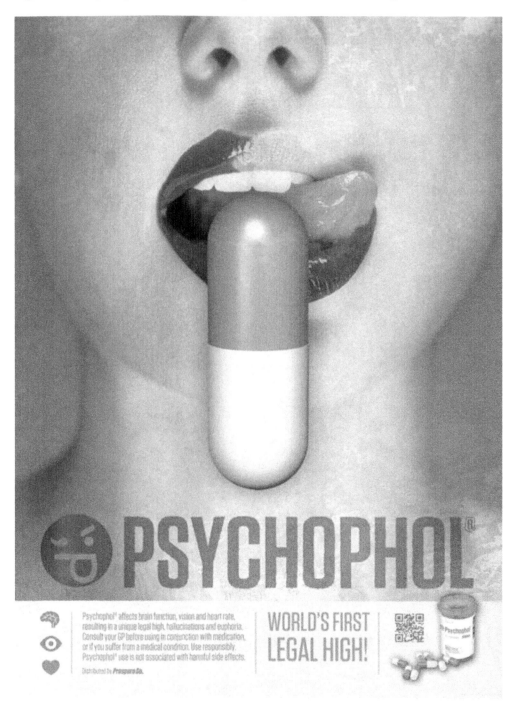

[81] Created by Santeri Lohi at BTL Brands.

7 CONTENT STRATEGY

This section provides advice about how you might determine the content you need and how you might have your audience co-create it with you. There's much that's missing here - particularly in the way of community management - but what there is I think is helpful. I've also included something on "viral video" which may seem a little out of place but I felt it worth including because it strikes to the heart of what makes content sharable.

When audiences connect well to your content, they go through three stages of engagement: Discovery, Experience and Exploration as shown in Figure 115.

Figure 115 Three Stages of Audience Engagement

The key to a successful content strategy is understanding (a) that there *are* these stages of engagement (b) what content is required for each stage and (c) what the goals are for each stage.

Failure to appreciate or acknowledge that there are these stages of engagement typically results in audiences being expected to do too much work too soon – which most won't do – and hence the content fails at the Discovery stage and the real experience never begins. Or, expositional-type content that belongs in Exploration is offered as Experience content and hence fails to engage because it doesn't tell a story.

Ignoring these stages is like expecting a kiss from a stranger before flirting with them or expecting to run off and get married after only the first date. Maybe in Vegas, but usually not anywhere else.

With transmedia, one media may act as Discovery content for another.   For example, the comic book serving as Discovery content for a movie or, in the example of the Xbox game *Alan Wake*, six webisodes act as Discovery content for the game.   However, it's important to remember that each media also has its own Discovery>Experience>Exploration stages as shown in Figure 116.

This is particularly important for indies who may think that creating a comic book for their movie will result automatically in an audience for their movie. It won't. The comic book first has to be discovered and experienced and it's only if the content is good enough will the reader begin exploring and "discover" the movie.

Note that I'm fond of encouraging an iterative approach to creating transmedia projects but here I'm also proposing a recursive approach: each and every piece of content should attempt to lure, convince and deliver.

Figure 116 Recursive Nature of Engagement

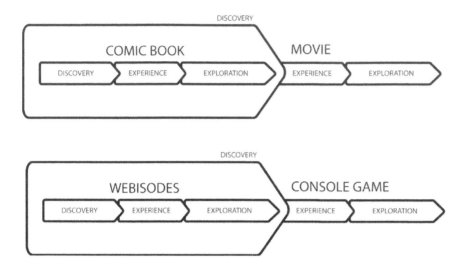

7.1 ENGAGING THE FIVE SENSES

Figure 117 uses the metaphor of sensory engagement to illustrate how audiences connect to your content. The concept is that audiences are at first suspicious of new content and that if we are to draw them in and lead them to the highest level of engagement – contributing to the canon – then we must resolve their reservations and satisfy their needs at each stage.

Figure 117 Engaging the Five Senses

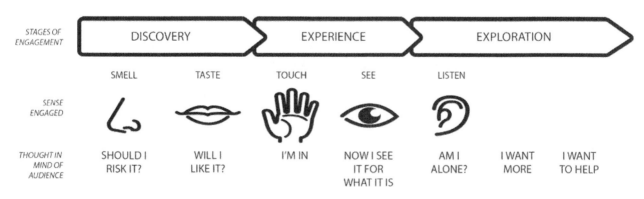

7.1.1 SMELL AND TEASERS

The first sensory stage is smell. The audience approaches tentatively and sniffs: is there a whiff of the familiar?

We are creatures of habit because evolution has shown it serves us well. Repeating past satisfying experiences is a successful strategy for survival in the wild and with entertainment it's a good indicator too.

The audience needs to be reassured that your content is worth its time and attention. You need to reduce the perceived risk by communicating "trustworthyness", "coolness", "quality", "appropriateness" – whatever values are sought by the audience for this type of project.

To communicate the correct values, I've created a content class called "Teasers". Of course the "teaser" is familiar to indie filmmakers – a 30 second or less video intended to bait the trap; not to explain or reveal too much but only to temp further engagement. In this model however, I've broadened the teaser into a full content category to include all content that can be digested with the minimal amount of attention.

Figure 118 shows the five content classes I've defined for each stage of engagement: Teaser, Trailer, Target, Participation and Collaboration.

Note that I had to create a name for the "target content" to avoid confusion with all the other content! Because of the recursive nature of this approach, any content might be at one time the target content and another time Discovery content.

Note too that because of the need to communicate quickly, visual clues from pictures, photos and web design are going to dominate the Teaser content class. But it's also the headlines you communicate: well-known cast or crew, one-line quotes from reviewers and so on.

Figure 118 Content Classes to Match Stage of Engagement

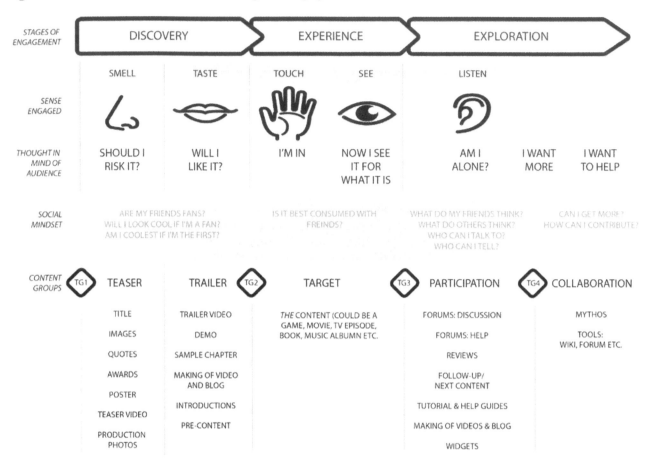

7.1.2 TASTE AND TRAILERS

If your project smells familiar then the audience can progress to a more specific, personal question: will I like it?

The teaser has convinced the audience your project is something they *might* like, but what can you tell them to reassure them it's worth their additional time and (possibly) money?

The movie trailer is a commercial. Its intention is to convince the audience that this movie is for them. In this model I've expanded the trailer to a class for all content that persuades. By which I mean content that removes the barrier between Discovery and Experience: it's the barrier between the *known* – the Teaser and Trailer content – and the *unknown* – the target content.

This barrier is represented by toll gate 2 – TG2.

7.1.3 TOLLGATES

In this model, tollgates are barriers between one stage and another.

TG1 is tollgate 1. It's the barrier that prevents audiences knowing that your project exists. TG1 can be breached by search engine optimization (SEO), recommendations, links and anything that puts your content on the map. But the first audience encounter should be with your Teaser content.

Tollgate 2 requires a little more explanation.

Think of TG2 as a wall that the audience must climb. Figure 119 shows how the project and business model will unavoidably create barriers to your content – some unintentional, some intentional.

Figure 119 Barriers to Your Content

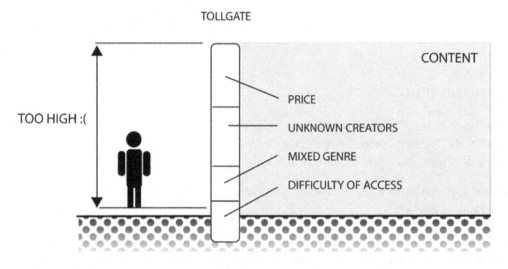

Content that you provide in Discovery helps the audience scale the wall – as shown in Figure 120. In this example, price creates a barrier to entry that of course can only be scaled by the audience paying the fee. However, the tollgate is far higher than solely the price and the audience will only part with its money once the perception of the tollgate is lower than the payment. Stated simply, buyers rarely make decisions not to purchase based on price – it's all those other barriers that have to be overcome first: value, suitability, risk, convenience, context and so on.

Figure 120 Overcoming the Tollgate

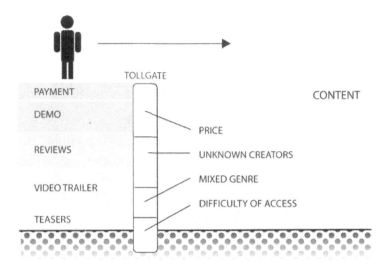

7.1.4   TOUCH AND SIGHT

It's only when the audience touches the target content that it can see it for what it is. If your Discovery content has done its job then the audience' expectations will be met or exceeded. But if you have deceived or misled them then they'll be disappointed.

There is nothing more you can do at this point. The target content is what it is. This is what the audience came for and it has to deliver.

After – though sometimes during- the Experience comes the Exploration. The tollgate TG3 is the barrier to be climbed to have the audience increase its *willing* engagement. Sometimes there can be confusion and this will lead to *unwilling* engagement: the audience experiences the content but doesn't quite "get it" and hence searches for an explanation or for help. In these situations of unwilling engagement, a high barrier at TG3 will lead to resentment.

Ordinarily we want the audience to engage further so reducing the height of TG3 should be a priority: make content easy to find and easy to access; signpost what content should follow the target content.

7.1.5   LISTENING AND PARTICIPATION

Although content in the participation stage may be available before the Experience, its goal is to aid exploration – not to tease or persuade (even though audiences might use it for reassurance to lower TG2).

Having experienced the target content – either in part or in full – the audience now listens for affirmation. They ask questions to themselves and to others and seek content that answers their questions or fulfils their desire for more.

Good content stimulates debate. Audiences want to discuss and share their experiences with others. They'll also want to extend the experience and will search for add-ons or new target content.

Some audience members will want to show their affiliation to the content by buying merchandise or embedding widgets; they'll want to encourage their friends to try the target content.

Content in this Exploration category is intended to reward and empower the advocate and to educate: it provides additional understanding and value to the target content. In this regard it may be acceptable to have "expositional" content such as character biographies, backstories and so on.

7.1.6 COLLABORATION

In this engagement model the ultimate audience engagement is collaboration or contribution. Not everyone in the audience will progress to this stage and some authors may think this undesirable.

Collaboration is not that same as participation. Participation might be passive (reading additional content and exploring the world) or active - voting, sharing, commenting, discussing, Tweeting and so on. Collaboration is adding to the storyworld: writing fan fiction, creating videos or illustrations. It's providing new content that you, as author, are free to embrace or reject.

Between participation and collaboration is tollgate 4 – it's a barrier created by the audience' perceived lack of time and skills, fear of ridicule and lack of information about how to contribute to the world. You can lower this barrier by providing tools, methods, encouragement and a supportive environment.

7.1.7 HOW TO USE THE 5-SENSES ENGAGEMENT MODEL

The premise with this approach is that a transmedia storyworld maybe too vast to expect an audience to jump right in. They have to be teased and led like Hansel and Gretel by a trail of breadcrumbs. Imagine your world to be a huge cavern – if you blindfold your audience and then first open their eyes once they're inside, the vastness is overwhelming – it's a new and scary place. Your audience needs orientation. They have to be guided through an entrance tunnel and see the cavern open up before their eyes and at their own pace. The more complex the world, the more handholding you need to do.

There's also the issue of the time, energy and cost required to digest a whole storyworld. Far better to give the audience smaller snacks at first until their appetite grows for larger, more time-consuming content.

Note that this content strategy is for audience engagement. When combined with the platform selection methodology, start first with revenue-generating target content and see how it might be prioritized by platform. Then use this engagement model to understand the relationship between the platforms and to identify additional content to aid Discovery and Exploration.

7.2 PLATFORMS

By "platforms" I mean the combination of media plus technology. So YouTube and iTunes would be two different platforms even if they can both deliver video. A printed book and The Kindle would be two different platforms. A cinema, a living room and an outdoor public space are all different platforms.

Almost any technology, medium and place can be used to convey your story but think about your audience again – what's their lifestyle? Where and how do they hang out? If you've got a story appealing to single-parent families is it likely they're going to attend live events? Maybe if it's during the day and they can bring their babies but most likely not in the evenings – they have problems with babysisters, cash and free time. Which platforms will appeal to this audience?

Think of your project as a lifestyle choice: it needs to slip into your audience' lives with the minimum amount of friction.

Now iterate back through the story. What might you do with the story to have it play out better across these platforms?

7.2.1 CONTRACTION, EXPANSION AND NAVIGATION

The biggest threat to transmedia projects is audience reluctance. The effort – both real and perceived – of jumping between platforms is something that really needs close examination. When problems occur it's usually because there's a conflict between what the producer or writer would like the audience to do and what the audience is prepared to do (or wouldn't do naturally). This can arise from commercial needs (e.g. to get from free social media to paid performance) but just as likely from artistic desire.

Many creators want their worlds to be "realistic" and assume that distributing their story across as many platforms as possible gives it authenticity[82]. This isn't always the case (as discussed in Section 2.6) and if you're faced with the choice of realism vs ease of use, go with ease of use if you want a large audience.

Figure 121 shows an example of the Communicator web-app which is our response to this issue of realism vs ease of use. The technology allows creators to simulate a fake mobile phone desktop and in doing so bring together common communication platforms into a single, manageable, private space. All the message feeds and content is hosted in Conducttr and then a special message type called Communicator Message is created by the creative and interpreted by the Communicator, open-source web software. This gives the creative huge powers to implement very simple or complex interactions without ever having to write any code.

Coders of course have the advantage that they can tailor the Communicator to look more unique and in

---

[82] Note that filmmakers learned a long time ago that to create an engaging experience doesn't require authenticity or realism. For example, a film about a woman going from inception of a baby to its birth is unlikely to last the full 9 months! Just the important bits will be shown and our imagination will bridge the gaps.

fact many have chosen to use the Communicator yet make it not look at all like a mobile phone.

A big advantage of the Communicator is providing the audience with navigation and feedback. This significantly reduces confusion and increases engagement... which increases immersion. Of course the web app still connects to the outside world so there's nothing to stop text messages or phone calls or ibeacons or views on a YouTube video from affecting the content in the managed environment of the Communicator and vice versa.

121 Conducttr's Communicator web-app

7.2.2 PLATFORM SELECTION

As I said above, by "platforms" I mean the combination of media plus technology. In this section I'd like to get you thinking about how you might go about selecting the *right* platforms. Of course there is no universal truth in platform selection – the *right* platforms are those that best suit you and the project. Although I would advocate that all projects have a community platform but that might not be part of your storytelling.

While keeping in mind the larger iterative development process, I recommend a similar five-stage iterative approach to selecting your platforms:

- Stage 1: go with your gut
- Stage 2: consider the relative strengths and weaknesses of each platform
- Stage 3: support the weaknesses of a platform with the strengths of others
- Stage 4: consider the timing of platforms relative to each other
- Stage 5: consider changes to the story to bake-in the platforms and timing.

7.2.2.1 GO WITH YOUR GUT

In the first instance, just go with your gut and list a few platforms that you think will suit your story and audience. This first pass will likely identify platforms based on the following:

- personal desire or bias
- experience
- popularity with audiences (including fashions and fads)
- ability to collect payment
- availability to find funding or sponsorship
- popularity with the press & bloggers (at certain times some platforms are more sexy that others)
- suitability to the story
- resources available.

Now take a closer look at each platform.

7.2.2.2 DETERMINE EACH PLATFORM'S STRENGTHS AND WEAKNESSES

In determining a platforms' strengths and weaknesses:

- first - consider the experience you'd like to create and which platforms are best suited

- second - rank the short list of platforms and ensure they create a mix that works synergistically

Choosing the right platform for the right experience

A senior executive at Yahoo spoke on Fora.tv back when I first wrote this book about how Apple asked Yahoo to design an app for the iPad that would be a "coffee table experience". The idea was that the iPad would be out on the coffee table in the living room when friends visited and the owner would want to pick up the device and share the Yahoo entertainment with her guests. Yahoo tailored its online content to suit the specifics of the iPad – not just the unique form factor but the unique consumption context too.

Device manufactures spend a lot of time thinking about how their products will be used. Learn a lesson from these guys and don't just partition your story across platforms but take time to adapt it so it works in the context of the device and the audience lifestyle.

Think of transmedia storytelling as an audience journey going from "wow" moment to "wow" moment. How and when do you get that "wow"?

Table 1 and Table 2 present possible ways to segment your platforms by the nature of audience participation. Use this type of approach to inform the platform selection around the type of experience you'd like to create.

Table 1 Possible platform segmentation 1

	Personal	Shared
"Passive" **(Lean back)**	Watching movie: mobile phone, laptop, tablet Reading: book, mobile, laptop, tablet, Kindle	Cinema TV Theatre?
"Interactive" **(Lean forward)**	Handheld game, Mobile, Laptop Tablet, Kindle (interactive fiction)	Multiplayer game Theatre? Tablet? – see comment above

Table 2 Possible platform segmentation 2

Location agnostic		Location-dependent	
Personal	*Shared*	*Personal*	*Shared*
Web series Comic/Graphic novel Motion comic Book eBook Pin (badge)			Poster Event Façade projection mapping[83]
Merchandise		Exhibition	
Mobile game ARG (alternative reality game) AR (augmented reality) Postcards and flyers			

Find the right mix of platforms

Given that each platform will have its own strengths and weaknesses, the goal of this stage is to be objective about why a certain platform should remain in the mix. My recommended approach is to score each platform based on the following criteria:

---

[83] http://www.youtube.com/watch?v=BGXcfvWhdDQ

- Revenue gained
- Cost (inc. time) of delivering content
- Ability of platform to enable social spread of content
- Fit to audience lifestyle
- Remarkability (uniqueness/coolness/timeliness/quality) of platform or content
- Timing of release to audience

The table below shows how these might be scored from 5 to 1 and Figure 122 presents an example from the Excel spreadsheet tool that's available for download at this book's website. To my mind DVD seems rather old fashioned now, 4 years on from when I first wrote this book, but I've left it in the table because it's illustrative of a particular project at that time.

While the exercise feels a little academic, if you have to justify external funding and justify to yourself that it's worth putting time into something, it's worth quickly running through the numbers – you might find some surprising results.

Table 3 Rating a Platform

	Rating
Revenue	Good=5, Poor=1
Cost	Low=5, High=1
Spreadability	Good=5, Poor=1
Lifestyle Fit	Good=5, Poor=1
Remarkability	Remarkable=5, Unremarkable=1

Figure 122 Platform Tool Example

Index	Vehicle2	Platform2	Revenue	Cost	Spreadability	Lifestyle F	Remarkability	Score	Weighting	Final Score
1	Novella	Kindle	5	1	0	3	2	11	2	22
2		PDF	0	1	5	1	1	8	1	8
3		Book	5	3	1	5	2	16	2	32
4		Text	0	1	5	1	1	8	1	8
5	Webseries	YouTube	0	1	5	5	2	13	1	13
6		iTunes	0	2	5	4	2	13	1	13
7		DVD	5	3	1	4	2	15	2	30
8								0	1	0
9								0	1	0
10								0	1	0
11								0	1	0
12								0	1	0
13								0	1	0

7.2.2.3 HAVE PLATFORMS SUPPORT EACH OTHER WITH CALLS-TO-ACTION

Now you know the pros and cons of each platform, you need to find ways to have them support each other. What I mean by this is that some platforms will be great for spreading awareness but lousy at making money. To combine the strengths of each platform means getting the audience to cross between platforms.

So how do we do this? Firstly it's important to remember that crossing platforms introduces friction. So rather than assume that audiences want multi-platform experiences, it's better to ask yourself three questions:

- What's my **objective** in having audiences cross platforms?
- How can I **motivate** audiences to cross platforms?
- What's the **reward** when they get there?

The Call to Action

Before I continue, I'd like to introduce a little jargon: the "call to action".

In web design, the button and wording on a page that asks you to "click here" or "sign up" is known as the "call to action" (CTA). It's a plea for the user to do something and good designers make these calls-to-action appear to be the default choice – you're nudged to take action through clear layout, positioning of the button, use of colors and so on.

The term is also used in advertising: "for a limited time only", "while stocks last", "a once in a lifetime offer". These are all calls to action to get you to do something *now* and not put off your decision.

A transmedia experience needs similar CTAs to get audiences to cross platforms.

What's the objective?

Part of your objective will be to create a fun experience but it will also relate to your business model. Here are three illustrations.

Example 1. A transmedia project has a comic book and a web series: the comic book will carry advertisements because it's believed that print advertising is less intrusive than pre-roll video advertising (because the ads won't get in the way of the story). The value of the advertising is such that it pays for both the comic book and the web series. Both will be given away for free but the advertiser has been promised a minimum number of comic book readers. Hence, it's important to get web series viewers to cross platforms to the comic book.

Example 2. A transmedia project has a mix of free and revenue-generating platforms: the free platforms build the audience and the revenue-generating platforms pay for the project. Your first thought might be that CTAs are needed to ensure the free audience migrates to a revenue platform. But this only provides part of the solution. Table 4 compares the relative audience sizes and revenue potentials across platforms and offers possible strategies to maximize the opportunities. Note that CTAs are used not only to grow revenue but to grow the audience - migrating them to more social platforms and providing spreadable content with CTAs to promote further growth.

Example 3. In my Lowlifes[84] project, physical and device-specific copies of the content is paid content

---

[84] http://lowlifes.tv

while web-based content is free. My primary, albeit weak, CTAs were:

- the project "logo" that displays three media types – informing audiences that this story spans multiple platforms
- the story in each media begs questions that the audience desires to be answered – and expects to find them in the other media; hence enticing them to cross platform.

With Example 3 in regard to moving from a free platform to a paid platform, I hoped that the friction of being tied to a desktop (free platform) will encourage supporters to migrate to a paid platform for a better experience more in tune with their lifestyle – for example, the ability to read a paperback book in the bath!

In these examples you can see that the business model creates different objectives for cross-platform traversal.

Table 4 Assessing your call-to-action: comparing audiences across platforms

		Audience Size and Loyalty/Enthusiasm		
		Casual Audience		Hardcore Audience
		Big	Small	
Platform Revenue	Biggest Revenue	Big Win. Keep the audience here and keep them spending! Refresh content, allow audience to create content (includes discussions, suggestions, live chat).	Provide CTA's to motivate audience to become Hardcore	Respect this audience: don't milk them for money. Use their enthusiasm to grow casual audience. Invest in community and provide spreadable content with CTAs to build wider audience.
	Smaller Revenues	Small Win. Can a gentle CTA motivate them towards a bigger revenue platform?	Provide CTA's to motivate audience to become Hardcore – more revenue will likely follow.	Maximize spreadability of content (see above). Provide gentle CTA to nudge onto higher revenue platforms.
	No Revenue	If revenue is important, need a CTA to send audience to a revenue platform	How is this platform contributing to the experience?	Maximize spreadability of content. CTAs to grow audience and nudge this audience to revenue platforms.

How do I motivate audiences?

Having decided your objectives, how do you motivate audiences to jump platform?

The one response to this question could well be "if you're having to 'motivate' audiences then surely that's highlighting a weakness in your experience?" I agree with that sentiment but if we'd like the audience to buy something or to be somewhere else for the next part of the experience then some motivation may well be required... just try to be gentle ☺

Digital content can have a nice layout and a URL to prompt action but what about live street theatre performance – how do you get audiences to cross platform from the street to, say, go online? Possible solutions to this example might be:

- flyers with your URL (potentially lacks social/real time web)
- flyers with QR code and Twitter id or phone number or email
- merch/pins (badges)/bookmarks and other give-aways with QR code or Twitter id
- performers wearing a t-shirt with a QR code or Twitter id or phone number or email
- the performers verbally encourage the audience to go online (e.g. shout at them!)

Figure 123 shows a great example of how to get in front of an audience. The image shows the front and back designs of an A3-size paper table mat laid out on every table in a café local to a location-based experience called the Rio PhoneHack[85] by ZU-UK. The mats are very enticing, offer something with low-effort to do from your seat (text "RIO") and then encourage you to leave your seat to go find the phones (which requires a little more effort).

Figure 123 Rio PhoneHack Table Mats

The bullet points above answer the mechanics of "how" and assumes that the live audience has mobile phones (so make sure the online landing page is small-screen friendly). But they don't address "why?"

Motivating the online involvement in this example ought to stress the urgency or immediacy of the situation – don't let the crowd disperse and hope they'll connect later: integrate the online component

---

[85] http://www.thespace.org/news/view/nell-frizzell-riofonehack

into the performance. Now you're incentivizing cross-platform activity with the promise of online participation in the live show.

If this isn't possible or appropriate, you need to consider other incentives ranging from blatant bribery with gifts or prizes to simply the promise of satisfying the audience's curiosity about what happens next or explaining what on earth the performance is all about.

Figure 124 illustrates a way to think about what you might need to do to motivate audiences to cross or combine platforms. The diagram shows the audience being acted on by two opposing forces: the incentive to migrate (positive force) and the disincentive to migrate represented by "friction" (negative force). By friction I mean anything that makes crossing platforms a pain: increased cost, additional keystrokes, diverted attention, low bandwidth and so on.

Figure 125 and Figure 126 illustrate the consequences when the opposing forces are of different magnitudes.

Figure 124 Incentive Vs Friction: Motivating the Audience to Cross Platforms

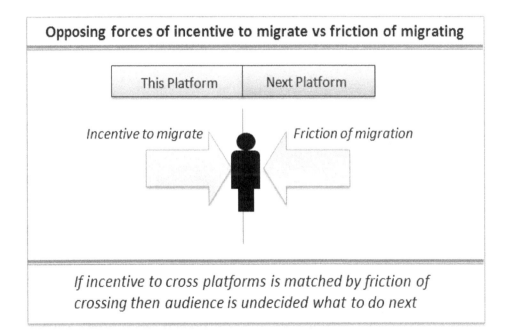

Figure 125 When Incentive > Friction Audience Crosses Platform

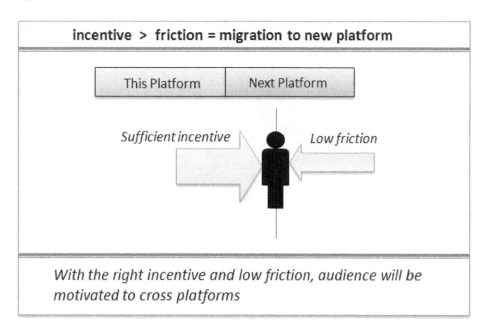

Figure 126 When Incentive < Friction Audience Doesn't Cross Platform

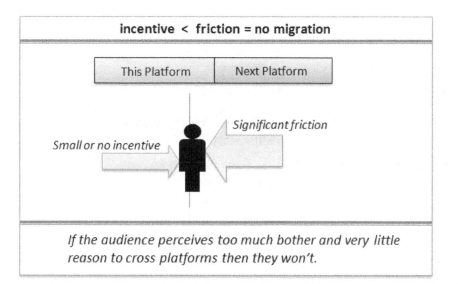

In the example of the street performance, the live activity creates attention and a call-to-action gets them online - but what now? Sell them a download? Get them to join a social network or mailing list? It's going to depend on where you are in the project and I'll address this in the next step.

7.2.2.4 PLATFORM TIMING

Unless you have unlimited resources it's likely you'll have to prioritize how platforms are released and to do that it will be helpful to define your objectives. Set your objectives with reference to your business model and resources.

Table 5 and Table 6 provide examples of roll-out strategies dependent on different business models. Note that steps can and may need to be combined or they may overlap. There's no hard and fast rule – the purpose of the approach is get you thinking logically and covering the bases.

Table 5 Example Platform Release Strategy 1

Step	Objective	Platforms
1	Have paid content available to capitalize on interest from day #1	Kindle, Pay-to-view, dowload
2	Release free content to build audience	Web series, comic book
3	Attract the hardcore audience	ARG with "secret" comic books and webisodes as level rewards
4	Work with hardcore to spread word to casual audience	Collaborative/co-created sequel

Table 6 Example Platform Release Strategy 2

Step	Objective	Platforms
1	Attract large casual audience	(sponsored & televised) flash mobs
2	Work to convert casuals to hardcore	Social network with unfolding/evolving Twitter story
3	Work with hardcore to spread word to develop experience	User-generated video & poster competitions
4	Sell paid content	DVD, merch, performance workshops/training

7.2.3 THINKING ABOUT MOBILE

When considering mobile as platform for transmedia storytelling, it's useful to imagine it as a window into the imagination. The mobile device provides an opportunity to reinterpret the real world and make the mundane part of a storyworld and vice versa, take a virtual world and overlay it onto the real world.

Figure 127 presents a framework for organizing your thoughts around how you might use mobile devices.

Figure 127 The five R's of mobile

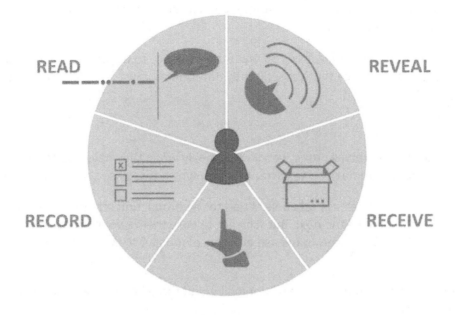

Read   In read mode, the device is used to decode surrounding information. This could be a QR code into a URL, an image into an augmented reality overlay or a GPS coordinate into a soundscape. The device is being use to translate cues into a story event.

Reveal   In reveal mode, the device is transmitting information about the individual or the surroundings. For example, an active story could learn about the person's location, their velocity or acceleration, their temperature, their mood maybe. Or, knowing the location, the device might transmit some contextual information such as local weather conditions, nearest ATM and so on.

Record   In record mode, the device is used as a personal journal to remember clues or characters discovered. Of course recording might happen automatically with the device logging places visited and quests completed. It's being used as a memory aid.

Receive   In receive mode, personalized or community content is delivered to the device by the active story. This could be badges and other rewards such as exclusive content or promotional offers. It might be purchases.

React   In react mode, the device owner manually signals intentions and desires by interacting with prompts.

7.3   DETERMINING YOUR RELEASE SCHEDULE

The release schedule describes how often you publish content to your audience. The goal is to profitably maintain engagement between published content. A good illustration of my approach can be given by looking at the webseries as a platform.

Core to my approach is understanding how you want the audience to engage with your story and then designing an integrated experience that consequently determines how each platform - in this case the web video - will be released.

***

Why do some web producers release their webisodes weekly when they have evergreen content? That is, if their series of web videos are not tied to current events, why not release them all at once?

One answer might be that the release schedule is tied to the production schedule - episodes are being produced one week and released the next. But why not release them two weeks apart or wait until enough episodes have been produced to release all at once or daily? Why not four hours apart or on demand?

My point is only that there should be some reasoning behind the scheduling and not just because TV has scheduled weekly content.

You see, if TV has taught us one thing about audiences, it's that they don't like to be kept waiting. They don't like to wait while the commercial plays, they don't like to wait while the episode downloads and they don't like to wait week-to-week. Many people record several episodes of a series before the viewing or they'll buy the complete series as a DVD boxset or season download. But of course audiences come to TV and the web with different expectations so why copy the TV model online if you don't have to?

I ask this of many producers and creators and the tendency to release episodically rather than in one release tends to be because it gives them something new to talk about; something new to mention on social media. My feeling is that it's still better to think about the audience first. If you have something highly anticipated or a campaign that requires delay of new information then sure, release episodically but otherwise I think it's better to capture the audience when you have them and have other content to release or implement a game or some other participation to keep the conversation going.

7.3.1   RE-THINKING YOUR WEB SERIES

This section looks at how you might optimize the release schedule for your webisodes. Core to my approach is understanding how you want the audience to engage with your story and then designing an integrated experience that consequently determines how the video will be released. There is no initial assumption that the schedule should be weekly or any other time period.

There is, I suppose, an assumption that most web series will have more than just the videos: there's usually a website, a blog, a forum, a mailing list, a Facebook page or some other mechanism that represents an opportunity to inform the audience of a new release and provide them with a backchannel. These additional non-video platforms are what makes your web series "an experience" rather than a series of videos. Even a single YouTube channel with the comments and likes enabled creates a participatory experience. Whatever the implementation, it is the experience that builds, empowers and engages your audience - it multiplies the draw of the video.

Here's a short list of considerations for determining the time interval between episodes with the key objective being to maintain engagement between episodes (i.e. you want audiences to watch the next episode):

- production limitations & opportunities

- distribution limitations & opportunities

- business model limitations & opportunities

- strength of story episode to episode (the narrative hook)

- need for the story to withhold information

- length of each episode (longer webisodes might benefit from longer periods between episodes to avoid overload)

- audience expectations and headroom (giving too much to consume between releases may lead to abandoned subscriptions).

7.3.2   MIND THE GAP: IS THE NARRATIVE STRONG ENOUGH TO BRIDGE THE DELAY?

Figure 128 illustrates how we'd like audience to move from episode to episode. In this example there's enough interest or engagement to have them come back for more.

Figure 128 Audience follows episode to episode

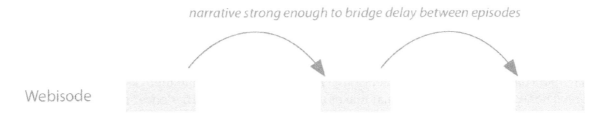

narrative strong enough to bridge delay between episodes

Webisode

Unfortunately there are a number of failure scenarios if the period between each release is wrong. In Figure 129, the audience abandons the web series because the content isn't strong enough to have them come back - there's not enough pull to bridge the gap.

In Figure 130, the audience is asked to work too hard to keep up and soon they find they're overwhelmed with content for the given schedule.

Figure 129 Abandons

weak narrative or incorrect release schedule causes orphaned episodes that are never watched

Webisode

Figure 130 Overload

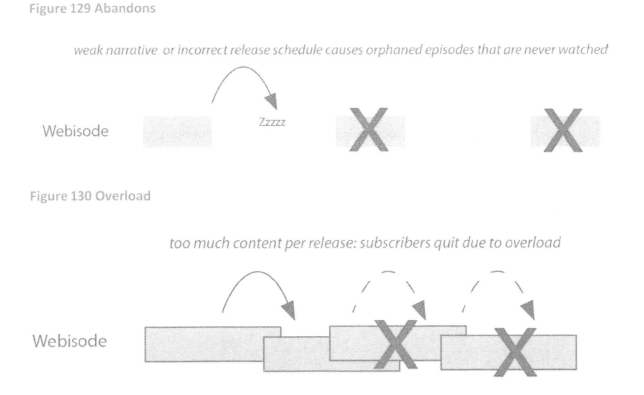

too much content per release: subscribers quit due to overload

Webisode

In both these failure scenarios one solution is to adjust or fine-tune the schedule - if that's possible. As I mentioned earlier, there may be reasons why you're stuck with the schedule.

Figure 131 Release schedule adjusted

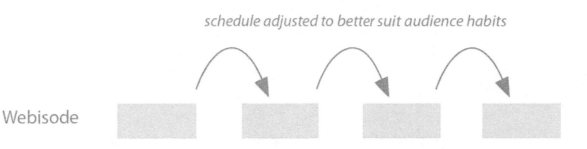

7.3.3   USING TRANSMEDIA STORYTELLING TO MAINTAIN ENGAGEMENT

Web series can be expensive to produce and the number of episodes is as likely to be determined by budget as anything else. This could mean you don't have enough webisodes to span the schedule you'd like or you need to maintain engagement between webisodes because the schedule is fixed.

Figure 132 shows how narrative spread to secondary, less expensive, media can be used to stitch together the web series - providing a mid-episode fix of story for those eager for more. The trick here is in the storytelling: to have the webisode and secondary media satisfying in their own right and hence consuming all media is optional which hence alleviates the chance of overload. Implied in the notion of "secondary media" is that it may indeed not stand alone and should be consumed as additional exploratory content (e.g. another optional layer).

Figure 132 Transmedia Storytelling applied to web video series

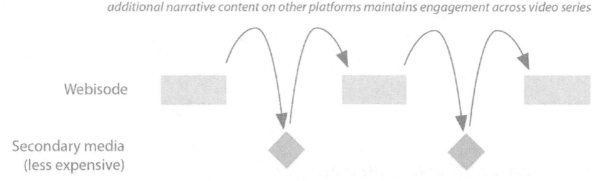

Figure 133 in contrast shows two equal media platforms both scheduled for episodic release but appealing to different audience sub-segments or consumption habits: e.g. media 1 is consumed while at work and media 2 consumed on the commute.

Here, each media has its own (intervening?) release schedule with additional narrative hooks and branches to take the audience to the next episode in the same media or to alternative media.

Figure 133 Native Episodic Transmedia Storytelling

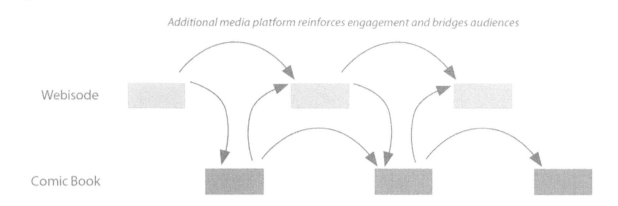

Additional media platform reinforces engagement and bridges audiences

Webisode

Comic Book

Finally of course, additional secondary media might be added to two primary media platforms - as shown in Figure 134.

Figure 134 Multi-layered Transmedia Story

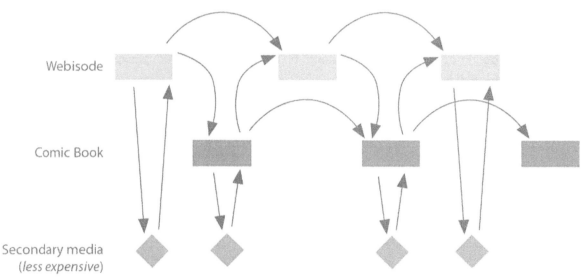

Additional media platform reinforces engagement and bridges audiences

Webisode

Comic Book

Secondary media
(*less expensive*)

7.3.4 ALLOW AUDIENCE TO GO WITH THE FLOW

So far I've assumed that all audience members are to be treated equally. But why not reward engaged followers with either additional content or early "pre-release" content? And if you do, does it matter that they might share with others ahead of the "proper" release?

I believe that when you have someone that's engaged you should allow them to ride out the engagement and see where it takes them. This means allowing them to request additional content on demand ahead of the release schedule which I further believe has the potential to turn engaged audiences to advocates - hence recruiting more audience.

YouTube's "Unlisted" video option is perfect for this: casual viewers won't see or find the video before it's made public but engaged audiences can be sent the link.

7.3.5 FACEBOOK'S EDGERANK

Although Facebook stopped using the term EdgeRank to refer to its news feed algorithm and the actual algorithm keeps being refined, the original equation is useful to examine.

An "edge" in Facebook jargon is what I might call a touchpoint. It's where someone touches a piece of content. The equation is shown below. Of course how it works is a mystery but the principals are worth understanding.

$$\sum_{edges\ e} Ue \times We \times De$$

Ue   Affinity score. How well connected is the content publisher to the receiver? This might be measured by how frequently you comment on each other's posts or how many mutual friends you share.

We   Weight. This is basically what type of content it is – text, an image, video – and how appreciated it is likely to be by the receiver. Typically you might expect that rich media like video is going to get a higher weighting than plain text

De   Decay over time. More or less how newsworthy is the content? New content is likely scored more highly than old content.

The principal understand here – which I think can be likely applied to any platform – is if you want people to see your content and share it, it's more likely to happen if its recent, has good production value and you have a relationship with the person you're sending it to.

7.3.6 LOWLIFES EXAMPLE

The first release of the project Lowlifes had three primary media: novella, webisodes and blog. I determined that it should be scheduled to be released two days apart over a period of 15 days or so. I felt that daily would lead to content overload and at three days the whole release would drag on too long.

One approach would have been to alternate the media - novella chapter on day 1, video on day 2, blog on day 3 and so on. But this would have incorrectly implied a sequence or priority to the media platforms that I was keen to avoid.

Consequently, at the same time content is made public, subscribers receive an email with links to the three media episodes plus the ability to request additional content from anywhere within the series. This would allow someone who was really into the videos, for example, to watch them all in one sitting by simply requesting them.

It's not a problem for me if someone grabs all the videos and posts them all on their own blog because my objective is to get them seen. It's evergreen content and within 3 weeks it would all be available in any case.

7.3.7   19 REINOS - A GAME OF THRONES IN SPAIN

For the fourth season of Game of Thrones in Spain, three of us from my company Transmedia Storyteller Ltd (TSL) – Belen Santa-Olalla, Eduardo Iglesias and I – worked with Canal+ Spain to create a transmedia experience that would build excitement leading up to the launch of the weekly TV series and continue until the penultimate episode.

The experience we created was called 19 Reinos[86] (19 Realms) and invited the audience to imagine that Spain was part of the world of Westeros. It was phenomenally successful with Canal+ presenting the results at SXSW 2015[87] that our work had created a 42% increase in positive brand sentiment (of which 23% was among a much sought-after younger demographic).

Our platform strategy was of course tied to the TV schedule but around that we had a lot of flexibility. The platforms were, in order of release:

- Live performance at which our fictional character – Edwyck - called to action 300 fans invited by Canal+ Spain to attend the filming of a TV trailer. Note that a few minutes before Edwyck's arrival we primed the crowd to get out their mobile phones so that they would be in hand and their thoughts would turn to using them. We gave the fans no instructions but at the same time we didn't want them to be apprehensive in videoing and shooting and uploading. This was the start of the digital campaign with a real world performance.
- Parchment. To further facilitate the cross-over from real world to digital world, as the fans left the live performance they were handed a parchment scroll that told them to email a fictional character to report any appearance of Edwyck who was a wanted man.
- Facebook was used as the community space
- A website was launched as the primary hub to content but it was to become the place to engaged fans to play...
- .. a massively multiplayer role-playing game (MMORPG) on Twitter. The game allowed players to

---

[86] http://www.conducttr.com/success-stories/19-reinos/

[87] http://www.slideshare.net/tstoryteller/game-of-thrones-transmedia-experience-19-reinos-for-canal-spain-sxsw2015

tweet instructions to @19reinos to attack each other but also betray, seduce and give away virtual currency.

- A 5-episode web series around the character Edwyck which introduced some of the strategy that might be useful in the MMORPG
- Partner websites were used to place weekly codes. The codes could be exchanged at the website for virtual currency. The currency was used to buy weapons, shields and potions

7.3.8   FLIPPING IT ON ITS HEAD?

It's very easy to think of the video content as the primary platform because it may have cost the most to produce. But if we put the audience at the center of the experience, we can re-image things – as shown in Figure 135 – where it's the interactive content that's the most important with the pre-recorded/pre-packaged content thought of as "cut scenes" to a larger participatory transmedia experience.

Figure 135 Episodic video when imagined as cut-scenes

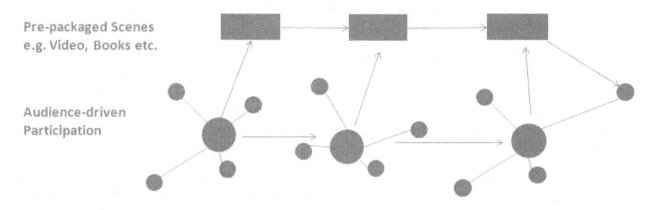

Pre-packaged Scenes
e.g. Video, Books etc.

Audience-driven
Participation

7.3.9   ANOTHER INTERATION OF STORY

Our objective throughout this process is to have the story and the experience of the story integrated with the business model.   Although you may have started with "the story" in mind, platform selection has rightly focused on "the experience". Now is the time to sanity check the experience and see if there's any missing story, story that now needs adapting or story + experience that can be improved.

For example, now you have a roll-out strategy for your platforms (the experience), iterate back through the story and look to improve or create new (in no particular order and please add more):

- Twists
- Surprises
- Cliff hangers
- Inciting incidents
- Reunions

- Breakups
- Conflict
- Discovery
- Exposition
- Reversals
- Suspense
- Threats
- Complications
- Conclusions

7.3.10 HOUSE OF CARDS – THE MISSED OPPORTUNITY

On Feb 1st 2013, Netflix released Season 1 of House of Cards: a 13-part TV show with every episode available from day one of release. At the time this release of all episodes at once caused quite a stir.

What follows is an essay I wrote at the time highlight what I thought to be the missed transmedia storytelling opportunities.

Watching House of Cards, it feels as though the script was written with transmedia storytelling in mind: real telephone numbers instead of those 555 numbers, a hashtag mentioned (#GoZoe), text messaging displayed as on-screen overlays, blogging journalists, many interesting peripheral characters that could have lives on social media to thicken the plot....   And yet none of it is realized.   Had I worked with this property, I would have explored deeper engagement & social conversation through the call girl (Rachel) who offers a quick win.

Three platforms are worth exploring: interactive text messaging - the easiest and most widely available second screen communication - plus interactive Twitter and Facebook commenting. Twitter is the most influential around show air-time while Facebook is more influential when the show is off-air - so it usually pays to do both.

Rather than simply deliver needless and unexciting character exposition as some transmedia executions do, text messages to Rachel could unlock a new subplot around the call girl and Doug Stamper. What is their relationship and how might this impact the Underwood-Stamper relationship we see on screen? When Underwood asks Stamper to use Rachel to destroy Russo or whenever Stamper is at an AA meeting... all of these moments could have been enriched.

This second layer of engagement would mean that whenever Stamper is on screen there are two audiences watching: insiders and outsiders. Few people like being an outsider and the emotional impact of having off-screen "private" knowledge (delivered by text) would really ratchet up the on screen drama. And this in turn generates additional online buzz on Twitter and Facebook.   If text messaging were deemed too expensive then Twitter direct messaging would work instead.

Imagine the engagement that this could produce for network or other episodic shows if Rachel were to text or tweet mid-week: a strategic call to action direct to every viewer that would build anticipation and speculation ahead of the next episode. For transmedia it doesn't matter that Netflix chooses to release all episodes at the same time because every household is watching (or not) at different times just as they are network shows thanks to DVRs and online services. The important thing is that the relationship between broadcaster/distributor and audience shifts from an impersonal one-to-many to a personal multiple one-to-one between a show character and each member of the audience. This is powerful and this example fulfils intrinsic human needs for connection, for significance and for autonomy.

And just think of the additional data...

In the early days of movie making, filmmakers thought that audiences would be confused if the film were edited. It took from 1895 until 1903 before someone cut the movie and edited it - that's 8 years. Today a similar debate goes on about transmedia storytelling. Yet audiences are becoming increasingly savvy about what constitutes a cross-platform call-to-action. It won't be long before it's common place to jump off the screen and into mobile/web based content and shows that don't do that will look very dated.. if they are watched at all.

7.3.11 SUMMARY

In summary then, if you assume that the audience always has something better to do with their time and money, it will absolutely focus your mind on maintaining engagement between episodic content and this will:

- determine the optimum release schedule (where you have the flexibility to choose it)

- highlight the need for a transmedia experience around an inflexible release schedule

- provoke a discussion about whether you should allow content on demand for the most engaged audience members or release all at once!

7.4   Crowdsourcing, Collaboration and Shared Storyworlds

Back in 2011 when the first version of this books was published, a lot of the concepts in this section were still in their infancy. There were some high-flying examples of collaborative platforms like WreakAMovie.com that has since stopped operating (it closed at the end of 2014) and some people debated if platforms like Kickstarter could become a sustainable financing model. I hope you feel that that question has been answered.

In the run-up to 2011, user-generated content (UGC) was treated with suspicion or contempt by some but today encouraging fan participation is an essential part of any campaign. It was clear to many back then that when storyworlds (i.e. intellectual properties) become popular, the appetite among fans for more content is almost impossible to sustain by the rights holder alone. Furthermore, fans understand the difference between fan-generated content and rights-holder generated content whether it's in terms of difference in quality or adherence to canon - and they accommodate both. And often very skilled artists and writers spend their free time working on passion projects for properties they love but have no commercial interest in.

Welcome to Sandition is an up-to-date example of user-generated content living harmoniously alongside the creator content (from Jay Bushman and Margaret Dunlap). The experience is an adaption of Jane Austen's unfinished novel Sanditon and played out across social media with video diaries forming the predominant mail.

What's interesting to me about Sanditon is that it's built around the technical capability of the Theatrics platform to allow fans to claim a "persona" – to become a character in the seaside town. Fans could role-play as their character and submit in-character video diaries of their lives in Sanditon. Theatrics had already shown success with Beckinfield[88] so there was a model to follow. Fans are thrown what I call "creative provocations" – a call to action that invites fans to provide their character's perspective on a certain development in the creator's story. This means that the creator gets to direct the fans and point them in the right direction but also to inspire them.

So what we see here is an unbracing of fan participation and enabled by a new technology – we have story, editorial and technology coherently integrated.

7.4.1 SHARED STORYWORLDS

"Shared Storyworld[89]" was not a term back in 2011, it was to be coined by Scott Walker to mean properties where the fans and the rights holder have a shared canonical interest and sometimes commercial. Or maybe I should use his definition:

> *an entertainment property designed to allow audiences/fans/consumers[90] to collaborate and participate in the creation of content for the entertainment property.*

The concept, then, is that the creator or rights holder says its ok for other people that he doesn't know to create work based on his work.. and importantly *sometimes* to be able to benefit commercially from their work.

A good example of a shared storyworld that allows commercial works is Clockwork Watch[91]. Creator Yoms has effectively created an open-source steampunk storyworld from which anyone may benefit financially should they wish to use his characters, locations, themes and such like. Haley Moore's Kickstarter project

---

[88] http://en.wikipedia.org/wiki/Beckinfield
[89] http://sharedstoryworlds.com/what-is-a-shared-story-world/
[90] That is, "unknown individuals"
[91] http://www.clockworkwatch.com/

Laser Lace Letters[92] is a story written by her, in the world of Clockwork Watch and told across multiple physical artefacts.

7.4.2 COLLABORATION & CROWDSOURCING

Although audience collaboration may not be a prerequisite for a transmedia project, I think we're at the point where the benefits of encouraging collaboration outweigh the problems[93]. The benefits I see relate to the fact that we now work in an overcrowded, competitive and often free content marketplace. Hence, collaboration for me means an opportunity to:

- test ideas and gauge support as early as possible and hence optimize investment of time and money – or give up early

- attract skilled, creative people to ambitious projects too big for either of us to tackle alone

- attract like-minded enthusiasts to help spread awareness in a win-win relationship rather than pestering friends to spam their friends.

So what's the difference between crowdsourcing and collaboration?

Crowdsourcing as implemented in commercial sites like www.99designs.com and www.audiodraft.com tend primarily to be a client pitching a problem in the form of a winner-takes-all competition with the winner receiving a cash payment. I'd argue that there's not much conversation going on here. Sure, the client asks a question and the crowd shouts back its answers but the crowd doesn't get to influence the requirements or bend the goals towards their needs.

Collaboration to me is more of a free-flowing exchange of ideas wherein the collaborator is able to influence the requirements; which for creative people importantly means a greater opportunity for self-expression. It's the reason why experienced crew might work for less on an independent production: a collaborator feels more like a creative partner than a work-for-hire.

The problem with "collaboration" is that it's more time-consuming to manage and there are issues of maintaining editorial control while still motivating collaborators. It's like directing actors: you have to know what you want without dictating how you get it. Collaboration is not for micro-managers.

But the fact that collaboration is more time-consuming actually works to the advantage of the independent filmmaker who is usually time-rich and cash-poor. Hollywood pays big bucks and they get to decide what happens when and how. Independents should be thinking laterally and using collaboration to leverage what little cash they have rather than struggle to find bigger budgets.

----

[92] http://www.laserlaceletters.com/
[93] I wrote this sentence in 2010 ;)

Why Bother?

Here are the reasons I hear most for involving the audience in the creative process:

- the crowd will spread awareness for you by word-of-mouth (i.e. social media) or through the "viral" nature of the task (i.e. getting their friends to vote or comment on uploaded videos, images, mashups etc.)

- the crowd (i.e. many people) will produce better or comparable results for less money

- crowdsourcing is still sexy enough that simply using the approach will generate publicity

- the crowd will produce new insights and being allowed to share their insights will increase their loyalty.

Opinions are divided on whether any or all of this is true; or whether it's ethical; or worth the investment; or worth the risk (perceived or real) of giving the crowd tools to participate only to have them used against you. Plus "professional" creative people argue that amateurs can't be expected to do what they do.

Those for and against can both present evidence in their defense but it seems to me that realizing the potential of crowdsourcing or fan participation is all about framing the participation correctly. And this depends on your objectives and on the crowd: both have to be aligned.

7.4.2.1   *RIGHT CROWD, RIGHT GOAL, RIGHT MIND*

The diagram below presents a framework for structuring your thoughts about what you might ask the crowd to do, what's in it for them and where you might find them.

Figure 136 Crowdsourcing Matrix

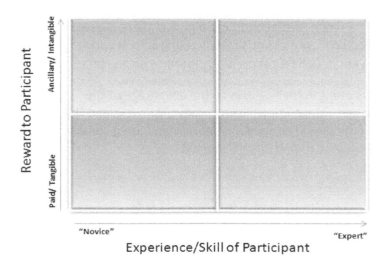

The axes I've chosen are:

- **Experience**. How skilled or knowledgeable does someone have to be to contribute something of value to you?

- **Reward**. What's the incentive or motivation for someone to take part?

If you think of this as "your requirements" vs "their requirements" then success ought to be where the requirements meet.

In the diagram, experience ranges from "novice" to "expert". What exactly constitutes a novice or an expert depends on the task and on your crowd. If you ask an established fan community to tell you which character ought to be killed off then it's probably safe to assume that they'll all be experts. But if you have no fan base to speak of, then even though you're asking the same question you need to assume they're novices.

As a participant, thinking of yourself as a "novice" or an "expert" is important because it determines how you perceive the complexity of the task you're being asked to do. Asking someone with no knowledge of After Effects to blur out a car license plate is a big ask. To someone with even a rudimentary knowledge of AE, it's child's play. Hence it's important to know your crowd.

Here's another example. What if you ask the same fan community to design a new logo for a starship? It's likely that within the crowd there's going to be a spread of abilities and some submissions are sure to be disappointing.   Does it matter that some of the crowd will submit amateurish or poor logos? I guess not if you get one usable logo you like – it only matters if no logos are useable and if you promised to use one of their designs.

With this logo design example, for audience involvement to work you have two options:

- include as part of the prize the prospect of having the fan's logo realized by a professional graphic designer. This would mean that you're more concerned with the process of engagement rather than the actual quality of submissions. It'll make more people feel like experts and hence more are able to contribute

- invite a different crowd – like the one at 99designs – where there's a higher probability of getting a usable design. But don't expect to see significant audience building and retention.

My point here is what's your objective? Is it to get a new logo? Or is it to engage or build a fan base?

7.4.3   DETERMINING THE REWARD

The second axis in the diagram is the reward. You might think that this ranges from "paid" to "unpaid" but that would be a little too simplistic.

Many people take part in crowdsourcing for higher motivational reasons such getting the bragging rights to say they won, getting a kick from others appreciating their work or maybe because they're building a portfolio or a resume. Perhaps it's just the fun of creating or taking part in something. Hence the upper range on the reward axis recognizes that the motivation to participate is more than the prospect of being paid: there are ancillary or intangible benefits to be gained. They might also be incentivized by the prospect of winning a cash prize but the motivation to spend a rainy weekend making a video comes not from the prize itself but from other intangible rewards.

The effect of increasing the cash or making the prize bigger is almost certain to result in more submissions. But increasing the ancillary or intangible rewards will also increase the submissions. If the prize is to have your video shown during the Super Bowl or on Saturday Night Live, then the kudos that bestows is more than having it air on an unknown small business website. Or having a commercial for Sony or Verizon in your portfolio is worth more in terms of enhanced reputation than… a commercial for an unknown small business.

You'll also get more submissions if you're asking the crowd to do less: because now there's a lower bar to clear and more of the crowd will feel capable enough to take part. It makes more of the crowd feel like an expert. But note that what you ask of the crowd is more than just to perform the task itself. It's also how much they are expected to read or agree to before they can contribute and what rights they give up with their submission.

Note too that it's important to balance what you ask of the crowd with the size of the possible reward. Ask too much for too little and not only is it unlikely to produce the desired results but it'll also look like exploitation.

7.4.4 STRUCTURING FOR COLLABORATION

Anyone that went to film school is sure to be familiar with those shoots where "collaboration" was taken to mean "everyone tries to do everyone else's job" – which of course results in conflict and disaster. Collaboration ought to mean me doing my job and trusting others to do theirs. But that involves appointing people in clearly defined roles with clearly defined responsibilities. The issue with audience collaboration or open participation is that it can become a free for all. Clearly, to prevent chaos there's a need for collaborators to have some form of guidelines and a structure for how and what they can contribute.

A great insight to these problems can be found in the Purefold[94] presentation by David Bausola, then of Ag8, in which he discusses the aims and needs of the project. David's collaborative transmedia framework has four pillars:

- Editorial: how the story develops with time and with collaboration

- Commercial: presumably how to meet the needs of the brands financing the project

---

[94] http://video.mit.edu/watch/case-study-transmedia-design-and-conceptualization-the-making-of-purefold-4889/

- Technological: how the project is implemented

- Operational: how collaborative input and responses to it are managed. Which for Purefold they hope to be close to real-time.

Another way to break down the problem may be to say that the four cornerstones to be defined for a successful collaborative project are:

- the process, which describes how contributors can participate

- the business model, which describes the financial incentives & rewards, if any, for collaborators

- the legal framework, which describes the contributor's rights and the project's rights

- the platform that supports the above.

One collaborative project worth checking out that has addressed these issues is a multiple media fantasy world called Runes of Gallidon[95]. The project clearly defines and explains:

- the process: contributors (Artisans in their world) must submit work for approval. Submissions are known as "Works" (complete standalone entities, like a short story, say) that contain "Ideas" (elements of the Work, like a character, say, or a location or spell). Only a Work counts towards the revenue share, Ideas are free for all to use

- the business model: if Gallidon makes money it's a 50:50 split for the contributor, if the contributor makes money then Gallidon takes 10%

- the legal framework: Creative Commons +

- the platform: email for submissions, a dedicated site to showcase contributions,   and an online forum for discussions.

Another example that made the 2011 version of this book but is now no longer with us was Wreckamovie.com which was a bespoke platform developed to support its collaborative process. Its cornerstones were as follows:

- the process: project owners pitch tasks; collaborators can "take a shot" which means submit an idea or the piece of work

- the business model: not immediately clear but I think no profit or revenue sharing was assumed

- the legal framework: select one from three Creative Commons licenses

---

[95] http://runesofgallidon.com/

- the platform: bespoke collaborative online software that accepts uploads, commenting, notifications and so on.

As a closing update to this section I strongly recommend checking out the amazing worldbuilding and fan collaboration in *Star Citizen* from Roberts Space Enterprises[96]. This storyworld started life as a phenomenally successful Kickstarter campaign (thanks to a bold concept and a premise that strong resonated with it audience: "pc games good, console industry bad") and has grown to enormous proportions thanks to its embracing, guiding and structuring for fan participation.

7.5   SPREADABLE MEDIA AND VIRAL VIDEOS

As the saying goes, if it doesn't spread, it's dead[97]. You need to design content that helps people tell their story... while telling your story; content that says something positive about the relationship between the giver and then receiver.

So first, let's define what I mean by a viral video. It ought to be a video that becomes popular because one person recommends it to their friends and they then recommend it to their friends and so on until the video views grow exponentially. So let's say a cool clip that people want to share.

There are those who argue a video is only viral after it's been shared or if it has several hundred thousand views. And Henry Jenkins argues that "viral" is completely the wrong word to use because it fosters the wrong mindset. But "viral video" has stuck with us as jargon and I think it's more helpful to look at "viral video" as a genre - just like music video or short film or feature film.

Note that:

- just uploading a clip to YouTube won't make it "go viral" and those popular clips from well-known brands all have additional marketing support (PR, paid advertising etc) and what's known as "seeding" - outreach to blogs and destination sites asking them to feature the clip.

- although this section exclusively discusses video, the same sentiments can be applied to all social media you'd like to be shared.

7.5.1   SO HOW DO YOU MAKE YOUR VIDEOS SHARABLE?

You have to put yourself in the shoes of the sharer and the receiver. Nobody wants to be associated with lame content, right? So don't create anything that's lame, self-indulgent, pretentious or badly acted unless it's for humorous effect!

---

[96] https://robertsspaceindustries.com/
[97] http://www.henryjenkins.org/2009/02/if_it_doesnt_spread_its_dead_p.html

Ask yourself these questions. When I send someone a link to this video (or other content):

- Will I look cool for sharing this video?

- Will it strengthen my friendship with the person I'm sending the video to?

- Will they look cool passing it on?

- Unless you can answer "yes" to all the above then revisit your video idea until you score 3 out of 3.

So here's my advice for optimizing your video to make it spreadable:

Spend more time thinking up a great idea than you spend shooting it. This will keep your costs down, keep your enthusiasm high and is most likely to yield the best results.

- Grab attention in the first 5 seconds. Be surprising, be funny, be shocking or tease. Just make sure you grab attention or else you'll be dead in the water.

- Finish with a punch line. There has to be a reward for anyone that's given you up to 30 seconds of their life! Make the last 5 seconds more surprising, funnier, more shocking or more provocative than the first 5 seconds. You want someone to finish the video and think "OMG I have to send this to …."

- Use the middle part of the video to engage. The part between the beginning and the end is the part that needs to keep evolving the idea or revealing something new. If you look at the Levi's viral Guy Backflips into Jeans[98], it's only about someone jumping into a pair of jeans but the team tries to keep the idea fresh by using different methods and places to jump. It's the same for the Ray-ban Never Hide videos.

Although there's no limit to how long your video can be, it's better to get in, do the job and get out within 30 seconds… 90 seconds tops. Sure, you'll find videos that are longer but you'll find that your time and money is better spent getting those 30 seconds the best they can be than making the video longer.

Invoke a primary emotion in the viewer. Think about which emotion you're trying to invoke in the viewer. Research on viral marketing from the Kelley School of Business at Indiana University found that the best emotions to invoke were surprise & joy. Others possible, although less effective, were sadness, anger, disgust, fear. Although not essential for the viral spread of your video, it's important for the client that the emotions invoked and the connections/connotations brought to mind are consistent with the brand's image and what their fans believe.

Don't make an advert: Your goal is to entertain, not to inform. An advert is different from what I'm defining as a viral video in that it has overt branding, slogans, product details. Virals are much more subtle

---

[98] https://www.youtube.com/watch?v=pShf2VuAu_Q

in their selling - they're entertainment first and a sales pitch a distant second. Creating a great advert is really tough to achieve and if you have limited resources or lack experience then there's a risk that your "viral" will look like a poor advert... which is unlikely to spread. So concentrate on making something entertaining that people want to share.

7.5.2   A NOTE ABOUT "INFLUENCERS" AND THE REST OF US

Influencers are those people assumed to be influential within their circle of friends or interest group. Many companies sprung up between 2011 and 2014 with various methodologies and technologies claiming to be able to identify influencers and reveal our own level of influence. I'm going to sidestep the question of what influence the influencer has and use the term to mean anyone with a large audience. In a world of fragmented attention spans and dwindling TV viewing, reaching a wide audience is tricky so reaching an "influencer" – someone with a large following on social media – and asking them to point their following in our direction seems like a good idea.

The quest for influencers and becoming an influencer is typical of the way that business is done. Many "YouTubers" with large subscriber bases now have their own agents broking deals with brands to get product endorsements and exposure. What's powerful about the YouTube star is that they have a relationship with their audience and received wisdom would have it that products need to be integrated into the show in an authentic way so that they don't lose subscriber trust. I agree with this approach of course but it'll be interesting to see how this is maintained over time.

If you're a major brand or someone with a lot of money or someone who also has influence then maybe you can approach influencers directly with a commercial proposition. An alternative common technique is to send interesting/amazing/intriguing gifts that will make for good unboxing videos or good photos – taken by the influencer and shared on his/her blog/video channel/twitter feed/Instagram/etc. Campfire's box of smells[99] for the Game of Thrones is a great example of this – a beautifully designed and packaged set of fragrances to invoke the world of Westeros. What Game of Thrones influencer would not want such a gift and love to talk about it?

The problem with trying to contact influencers is that everyone else is likely trying to contact them. So getting a response or willingness to help could be unlikely. But here's an interesting insight... influencers can only retain their following if they remain relevant. If the following is talking about a movie or a game and the influencer isn't then he/she appears out of touch. So it is possible that a groundswell of interest among "the following" can send a powerful message to the influencer. This happened with Kony, Susan Boyle and Gangnam Style – all had a groundswell of support among the following which caused them to come to the attention of the influencer (respectively Opra Winfrey, ABC News and Robbie Williams).

---

[99] http://www.geeksofdoom.com/2011/03/02/doom-deliveries-scents-scrolls-box-from-hbos-game-of-thrones

7.5.3 VIRAL VIDEO STYLES AND FURTHER TIPS

As the world of viral video evolves it's possible to see some similarities among the types of content that's popular online. Note that the styles are not mutually exclusive which means a video's spreadable potential is often helped by combining several styles.

Here are the styles/models I've identified:

- Repeat & innovate: keep it fresh

- Do This at Home/Mash-Up

- How Did They Do That? Did They Really Do That?

- Outrageous (ly Funny)

- Sensational Story

- Surreal

There's also a short discussion here, Cool But Not Viral?, about why these popular videos are not "viral" in the definition I've given above.

7.5.3.1 REPEAT AND INNOVATE: KEEP IT FRESH

Videos that fall into this category are the Levi's Guy Backflips into Jeans and the Ray-ban video Guy Catches Glasses with Face[100]. The Levi's viral is only about someone jumping into a pair of jeans – each jump shown as one shot - but the team tries to keep the idea fresh by using different methods and places to jump and different angles. The idea (of jumping into jeans) is big enough to sustain several iterations. Ditto with Guys Catches Glasses with Face but note how in both the videos the best feat is saved until last – it's the pay-off, the reward for watching until the end.

Both of these videos have the Did They Really Do That? engagement too which prompts viewers to stop, pause and rewind the video – spurring conversation and more sharing.

Thorton's "Stuck[101]" by Harmony Korine is also in this repeat and innovate category but rather than go for amazement and laughs, it's wonderfully touching and by returning to the boy on the bench we get the sense of a story unfolding. The limitation of Stuck is that it creates a warm feeling inside rather than the uplifting rush of success (as with the Levis and Ray-ban videos) and this potentially contributes to less sharing.

---

[100] https://www.youtube.com/watch?v=-prfAENSh2k
[101] https://www.youtube.com/watch?v=QrQN2-WShGQ

7.5.3.2   DO THIS AT HOME/MASH-UP

The benefit of a simple idea or a very clear concept is that viewers can spoof it, parody it and mash it up to produce spin-offs that further spread awareness of the original video.

For an example in this category, take Cadbury's Eyebrows[102]. It's impossible to watch and not feel invited to move your eyebrows as the two kids do! Not only does it offer excellent potential to parody with different music and/or different characters but it also invokes the Did They Really Do That question - don't those eyebrows move to fast not to have been enhanced with computer graphics?

A more recent example is Gangnam Style[103] the massively shared video which at the time of writing has 2.3 *billion* views on YouTube. Sure there's a catchy tune and the absurd locations & costumes but this begs people to copy the dance moves. In an interview with the New York Times[104] and other places says that he spent a month working on the horse dance moves and more in addition so that the moves could be copied.

The thousands (millions?) of Ice Bucket Challenge videos became a phenomenon not only because a referral mechanism was built into the experience ("I challenge Rob, Stacy, Jenny..etc.") but because this was something we *could* do at home and all had surprising endings – either the drenched person's reaction or sometimes ending in a funny catastrophe.

7.5.3.3   HOW DID THEY DO THAT? DID THEY REALLY DO THAT?

Kobe Jumps Over Speeding Car[105] doesn't have a powerful grab in the first 5 seconds but because it's Kobe Bryant, it's his celebrity and the promise of the video title that gets us hooked. Then he jumps the car and we wonder, did he really do that? Whenever you can provoke a comments war about whether the clip is "fake" or "real" then you've engaged an audience!

I've also included in this style T-mobile's Life's for Sharing[106] although in truth it's a combination of many styles. For example, it's surprising, it follows the Repeat and Innovate model - frequently changing songs and dance moves to keep it fresh, it begs the How Did They Do That? question to stimulate conversation and further enquiry, it even has a just little of the Do This At Home going for it. It's main failing is the weak primary emotion (wonderment) and the lack of a punch line. However, the strength of the Repeat & Innovate and the How Did They Do That? vibes probably overcome the weaknesses but even so, when everyone stops dancing and walks off it's a bit flat after all the energy in the video.

---

[102] https://www.youtube.com/watch?v=TVblWq3tDwY
[103] https://www.youtube.com/watch?v=9bZkp7q19f0
[104] http://www.nytimes.com/2012/10/14/arts/music/interview-psy-the-artist-behind-gangnam-style.html
[105] https://www.youtube.com/watch?v=BlWeEFV59d4
[106] https://www.youtube.com/watch?v=mUZrrbgCdYc

7.5.3.4   OUTRAGEOUS (LY FUNNY)

The perfect example of this is the Durex Get It On[107]. This viral scores on so many levels: it's funny because it's taboo (sex, animal sex) yet cute (balloon creatures) so doesn't become gross-out funny and it's technically cool and makes viewers ask "How Did They Do That"?

I've also included in this category a music video for the group Make The Girl Dance[108]. Although not outrageously funny, it's outrageous in the sense of three women walking nude through Paris! The video works not just because of the nudity but because it's excellently executed in one continuous shot (very difficult to achieve), it innovates with different girls, it's humorous & engaging to watch at the bystanders' reactions and it's amazing that they got away with it!

7.5.3.5   SENSATIONAL STORY

For this format to work, at its heart there has to be a story that generates conversation around the water cooler - it has to be a sensational story. It's the kind of tale that passes for "news" in the tabloids and gossip magazines - we know it's unimportant but it's fun to talk about. The stories might provide light-hearted "humorous shock" and there's often a sense of schadenfreude (which kind of means laughing at someone else's misery).

This is a tough category to get right. A great example is the video below for Triumph Boats[109]. It looks like a candid clip because it's taken in one shot, the picture quality isn't so great and at the end the camera operator runs away leaving the camera running. But it was actually created by an ad agency to highlight & promote the strength of Triumph's boats.

Another, less effective example, is Leaked Assassination Footage[110] from Russia for the video game MIR-12. The problem with this "viral" is that it doesn't invoke any strong primary emotions and it isn't surprising or shocking enough. It succeeds in part because it has a "Did They Really Do That?" interest: it makes the viewer consider if this is actually real footage (although it had us immediately shouting "fake" - the acting & action is too poorly staged and executed to look "realistic"). It's doubtful that this video was actually shared among many friends.

I would also include her the Susan Boyle video of her first appearance on TV. Note that this video is expertly edited to build the story in the "zero to hero" mold – first the snarky unpleasant bullying that these shows unfortunately relish, an expectation that she's going to be rubbish and then of course our prejudices are revealed for what they are, that we do judge a book by its cover. This is a sensational true story that ends with an enormous feeling of well-being (mixed with a little shame I hope) and a desire to catch our friends off-guard and share the uplifting resolution with them.

---

[107] https://www.youtube.com/watch?v=Uqt3Zb7BltA
[108] https://www.youtube.com/watch?v=uHF3X8tQYPU
[109] https://www.youtube.com/watch?v=tMCVIlOD9UY
[110] https://www.youtube.com/watch?v=6FGsvOzB1Hk

7.5.3.6   SURREAL

This is my last category and ought to be used with caution. It's very easy to say "my video is surreal" when what really ought to be said is that it's confusing! In many ways, most viral videos have some surreal quality to them but it's worth looking at a couple of the best examples.

A classic example of this style is Cadbury's Gorilla[111]. This viral was so ahead of it's time that it generated incredible off-net conversations around the water cooler that further fueled its online growth. More than just surreal though, the video is inventive, engaging, humorous and touching. Investing the gorilla with human traits gives us a warm feeling inside but it also acts as a hook to keep us engaged and in suspense wondering what's going to happen.

Still great but a little less successful is Ray-ban's Cow Gives Birth to Dude[112]. Although it's surreal, it's surprising, it's humorous... it lacks a real feel-good vibe or laugh-out-loud punch line. Massive Yarn Ball Rolls Through San Francisco[113] is better although in a similar vein - it's cool, it's surreal, it's makes you smile but the punch line could just be a little better.

7.5.3.7   COOL BUT NOT VIRAL?

There are many (award-winning) commercials that get shared on the Internet but that doesn't make them a "spreadable". For example, Air New Zealand Nothing to Hide[114] creates a stir because of the nudity/cheekiness and it's certainly inventive but the overt branding and advertising limits it's spreadability - how many more people would have forwarded this video were it not an advert?

The same can be said of Gucci's Flora[115] by Chris Cunningham. Again it's a wonderful video but it's not a viral. Quite apart from the fact that it ends on a pack shot, it doesn't invoke a strong enough primary emotion - joy maybe but it's more of wonderment than happiness.

---

[111] https://www.youtube.com/watch?v=TnzFRV1LwIo
[112] https://www.youtube.com/watch?v=3E-pHMN4DyA
[113] https://vimeo.com/4482052
[114] https://www.youtube.com/watch?v=DZRmcKX85so
[115] https://www.youtube.com/watch?v=v3KXWUvvjo8

8   THE REVENUE MODEL

Pulling in an audience is tough and pulling in finance is tougher. This section discusses:

- the transmedia business modelros
- audience-pays financing
- sponsored financing:
    - branded entertainment
    - crowdfunding

8.1   THE TRANSMEDIA BUSINESS MODEL

In the "old days" (Figure 137) raising finance was what you did first. You needed that money to make the movie and then you'd sell the movie to a distributor whose job it was to sell it to the audience. Hell, you might even get presales in which case you'd killed two birds with one stone.

The important point from this is that as the filmmaker you only had to convince a limited number of people (investors) that you had a movie worth making (because it would make money). *You didn't have to convince them it was worth watching.*

One reason you didn't have to prove you had an audience waiting to see your movie was because it couldn't be proven. Instead, one might use (often bogus) comparisons with other movies and of course, whenever possible, outliers like *The Blair Witch Project* or *Fahrenheit 911* or *Sideways*.

When the finished movie failed to find an audience it was the distributor's fault. They didn't know how to position the movie correctly. They didn't spend enough money on P&A[116]. The box art was bad.

Figure 137 The Old Model

Having worked with our distributors in some markets and selling directly at some horror conventions, it's

---

[116] Prints and advertising. This is the money spent getting the movie into cinemas on 35mm film and having an audience show up to watch it.

very sobering to get a firsthand experience of audience expectations:

Me: It's about love and sacrifice and how you don't notice you're onto something good until it's gone.

Horror fan: Great. How much T&A[117] is there?

8.1.1 THE NEW MODEL

When MySpace, Facebook, YouTube etc. arrived it became possible to raise awareness of the movie and start building an audience before the movie was released. But still it felt like something peripheral to the marketing of the movie. The audience building was an industry-side activity that you could take to the distributor with your one-sheet and your reviews: look we have several thousand fans. Most of whom in all likelihood were other independents flogging a movie or a book.

Today, most filmmakers – maybe not readers of this book – but most filmmakers still have the mindset towards social media that it's a new spam tool. Look, now I can pester people to be my "fan" and I can get them to pester their friends to be my "fan". Please Digg me up. Please Stumble on me. It's the worst kind of networking: "please help me" they bleat.

Worst still can be the crowdfunders: "please give me money".   I'm not against audiences paying upfront – as with the Kickstarter model – so it's not the principle, it's typically the execution I have a problem with (which I address in the section on Crowdfunding! Page 191).

And I totally believe in the power of social media but I don't like it when it's so often used in an unproductive, disappointing way.

So enter the new model of filmmaking (Figure 138):

- there's a genuine affection... nay, anticipation... between the audience and the movie

- the affection is leveraged to pre-sell to the audience while still raising finance in the traditional way

- when the movie is available for viewing, it might be that only a subset of the audience will pay for it. So they'll be simultaneous free exhibition and sales.

Back it 2011 it was easy to be skeptical that millions of dollars could be raised via crowdfunding but now it's been proven possible. Even so, the repeatability of the model for the same creative is still tricky to pull off and requires considerable dedication to the community. What I've learned in the years since the first book is that when you crowdfund, you're empowering the fans and helping make something for them – which hopefully coincides with what you want to make for yourself. It's not about your dream, it's about

---

[117] nudity

theirs.

Figure 138 The New Model

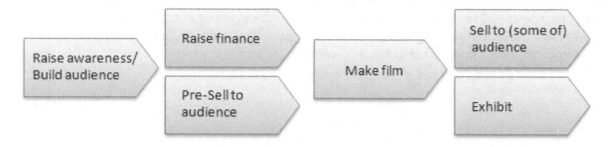

My change of mindset then is not to think of this as audience building but rather community finding – where's an existing fan base that would want you to create something for them?

8.1.2   THE TRANSMEDIA MODEL

Raising awareness and audience building is tough. It's tough enough when you have a finished movie but try doing it for a movie that's yet to be made.

That's why we need a transmedia model for filmmaking in which the filmmaker uses his own money to make some (low-cost) content to build an audience ahead of doing anything else.

There's long been a school of thought that says to get finance for your feature you should shoot the trailer or shoot a short film based on the feature. I know this can work but I've never been a fan of this approach if only because I know finance is most often raised without it.

What transmedia storytelling offers however is not the Cinderella story of "big investor swoops to finance movie" but a genuine, low-cost, grass-roots audience building.

Right now, (online) comic books seem to be the order of the day – offering an excellent way to engage audiences in the story and show some visual flare or at worst nice eye candy to grab attention[118]. But there's lots of untapped potential for many other participatory experiences and content both online and offline. Note that the content has to have value. It can't be a trailer or marketing fluff – you have to produce the real McCoy if you're going to capture audiences.

In the transmedia business model, the financing, exhibition and fundraising work together in tandem with

---

[118] Here's a nice example http://exoriare.com/

the potential for the feature film to become self-funding. Remember that it's not all for free. Free is your loss-leader to generate the money. Even if it's "real content" you might still effectively look at it as a marketing cost – it can help to position it in this way to investors. And note that what's free and what's paid will be in flux – maybe changing over time and from media to media.

So in the ideal scenario the filmmaker bootstraps the movie with the low-cost media, the website, presumably some merchandise but then it's up to the audience to decide what happens next.   The filmmaker will use a basket of financing initiatives: free, pre-paid, paid, paid+[119], investment and sponsorship (including brand integration/product placement) to finance the movie.

Figure 139 Transmedia Business Model

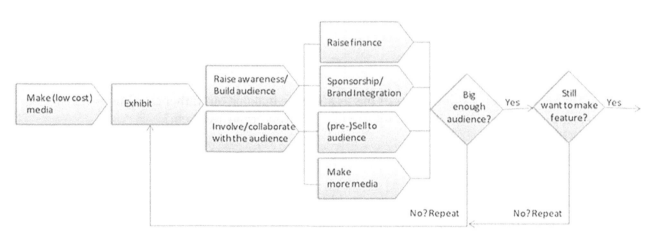

This model has several implications:

- If you do it right they'll be demand for more content... which maybe you can't afford to make in the early days. Or at least can't afford to make alone. And that's why collaboration of all kinds is important to the indie – with audiences and with other filmmakers.

- Sponsorship in the form of cash (rather than products for free) from brands won't solely go to properties with big audiences. If your story reaches the audiences that other marketing finds hard to reach then that's going to work too. The one significant problem I can see is that few brands want to be associated with edgy content... unless it's "edgy" in the *Green Day* plastic-punk, manufactured sense rather than the raw, confrontational *Crass/Poison Girls/Flux of Pink Indians* edgy. Counterbalancing this is fans who may appreciate that you've rejected the brands... maybe.

- Filmmakers still need to become familiar with audience needs and learn how to captivate them. It won't be anyone else's fault that you don't have an audience. There's no opportunity to finish the movie and then throw it over the wall to someone else to find the audience for it.

---

[119] Paid+ is where buyers can opt to pay more than the base price – usually via a drop-down menu of price points.

- Free media is a feeler gauge: collect comments, listen to feedback, evolve the feature to meet the audience expectations.

- It's going to be a long commitment to the audience so be sure you pick a story you really want to tell.   Indies that follow this transmedia model will be offering an evolving service rather than a one-off product and that means audiences become customers that need to be listened to, responded to, cared for and managed.

- If you perfect this evolving transmedia ecosystem you may ask yourself if you still want to make a feature after all.

A final sobering thought: I know we'd all like to believe that story is king but audiences will only discover the story if you hook them in. Don't expect anyone to delve deeply into your storyworld looking for brilliance. You have to provide "satellite media" that orbits the core: it's easy to digest and looks cool or fun. Celebrity cast or crew and genre are going to get attention and convey credibility – just as they always have.

I've illustrated this in the figure below where I've taken the sales funnel model and used it to illustrate how you want to pull in audiences, turning casual interest to hardcore repeat purchases.

Figure 140 Matching Content to Audience Commitment

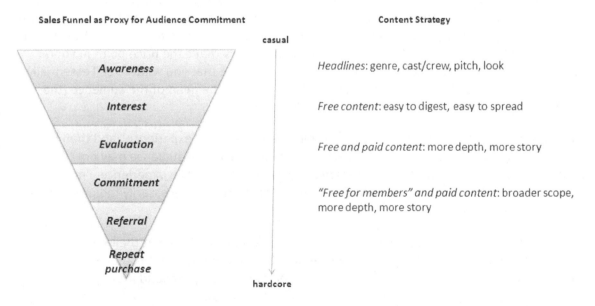

To summarize then, I'm advocating that creative people move to transmedia storytelling because it's the way you build audiences. And building an audience will unlock the financing – either from fans, sponsors or investors.

8.2 Audience-Pays Financing

With Audience-Pays financing, you're asking the audience to pay for what they consume. Today it feels like an old fashioned idea ☺

The biggest problem with audience-pays financing is that it leaves the creative vulnerable to a market that has increasingly shown itself unwilling to pay (or at least pay to the degree we'd like). I think most would agree that the situation is bad for the traditional model of make-something-and-sell-it-to-everyone-at-the-same-price and it's given rise to a range of pricing models including rental, subscription and pay-what-you-can.

Possibly the most influential ideas to the problem of getting people to part with money when they can often get your content for free are Kevin Kelly's "Better Than Free[120]" and Mike Masnick's now famous equation:

Connect with Fans + Reason to Buy = $$$[121]

I won't replicate the content of the blog posts I've referenced in the footnotes except to say the main concept is that you must socialize with your audience and sell them something they *value*. The key to success is finding what it is they value and pricing it correctly.

Unlocking the value means understanding your audience and understanding the competition from other products and services. You may feel very strongly that if a video or artwork takes 5 days to complete and you rate your time at $1 per day that you're justified in asking for $5 plus a margin, so say $7. However, if similar products are widely available for $3 (or free) then unfortunately that's the price point in your audience's mind. You must therefore sell something different. It may be that you want to sell essentially the same physical product but you need to find that additional value in the mind of the audience (the consumer) so that they are prepared to pay the $7 you'd like.

In Figure 141 I've worked with the idea that you might sell a "thing" and an "experience" and then looked where the audience might perceive value. So, for example, while some of the audience may not buy a regular download perhaps they might if it were personalized in some way. Or, in experience, I'm suggesting that a patron is effectively buying a feel-good experience and not necessarily the product they download or hold in their hands.

A simple example of how your audience might perceive value differently is to look at their balance of leisure time and disposable income: young people will tend to have more leisure time and less money while older audiences may value their time more and hence be more willing to spend money for convenience.

All of these ideas and approaches are relevant to crowdsourcing actually when it comes to deciding what

---

[120] http://www.kk.org/thetechnium/archives/2008/01/better_than_fre.php
[121] http://www.techdirt.com/articles/20090719/2246525598.shtml

tiers and rewards to create because my view is that they can appeal to these different segments of your audience.

Figure 141 Connecting with Fans and Understanding What they Value

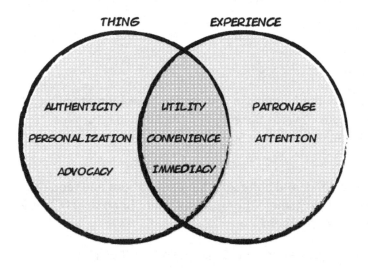

8.3 Sponsored Financing

With sponsored financing the project is paid for by someone other than the audience consuming the project. I've included in this section:

- product placement and sponsorship

- branded entertainment

- crowdfunding.

8.3.1 WHAT IS A BRAND?

The word "brand" is often used by filmmakers as a short hand for "well-known company". But in marketing terms and the way companies think about "their brand" is much more than that.

To a company, their brand is the sum of all the conversations and opinions that people have about them and their products. "The brand" is the emotional and psychological response from customers when they hear the company's name or see the company's logo or products.

Coke and Pepsi are very similar products but their names illicit very different thoughts, feelings and opinions. That difference is the result of branding. When branding is done well, it's not only what the company says about itself in adverts, it's about how customers are greeted in stores, how the products look and feel, how suppliers are selected and handled.   For example, a coffee shop or supermarket that sells FairTrade products is communicating more about its brand values as any commercial it might produce.

Given the money and time it takes to create a brand – the feelings and associations in our minds when we think of a particular company – you can perhaps appreciate the concerns a brand manager might have with branded entertainment.

8.3.2   PRODUCT PLACEMENT & SPONSORSHIP

Product placement – having a company or product used or featured in your movie – has long been sought after by indie filmmakers hoping to have companies pay towards the cost of production in return for exposure. Newspapers often zing with speculation about how much Sony, Omega or BMW paid to have their products feature in the latest James Bond movie[122].

Unfortunately most indie productions are not James Bond. And although your expectations and requests may be modest, the major brands are much more likely to gamble the house on James Bond than flutter a few pennies on an indie production – it's just a safer bet for them.

Fortunately all is not lost if you're flexible with your requests and you think local rather than global.

Public relations is important to most companies as is "corporate and social responsibility" (CSR). You'll find that the big companies in your area support many initiatives aimed at fostering the support of the local community and reinforcing the feeling among employees that this company is a good one to work for. Support under the banner of PR and CSR might be sponsoring local fates and fairs, having a float in the local parade, sponsoring the local soccer team or ballet troupe and it could also be your transmedia project.

And it's not just big businesses - many smaller, local businesses rely on the support and awareness of the local community. Your selling point is not a global YouTube audience - it's the local exposure and local goodwill generated.

For these local companies, product placement maybe not be a requirement at all and a simple "thank you" on the credits or on the publicity materials will do. In fact, you might find that a local company will sponsor a screening, or the publicity for a screening, or give you a product that you can use as a prize to help with driving awareness of your project.

In fact, cash is incredibly hard to get but asking for products and "soft" support is much easier and very often likely to get a "yes". For example, for my movie *London Voodoo* we had the following support:

- Orange UK the mobile company gave us 12 mobile phones with free calling between the mobiles

---

[122] http://www.theguardian.com/film/shortcuts/2014/dec/16/view-to-a-sell-james-bond-product-placement-boost-profile

so long as we had a close-up of a phone they were keen to promote

- Subaru gave us two cars to use for the duration of the shoot so long as our hero had one as his family car.

And other productions I've worked on have had free food from fast food outlets.

Although we honored our commitments, nobody from those companies ever came to check and although it wasn't cash support it certainly had a direct impact on our budget.

8.3.2.1   BUILDING ALLIANCES

The one thing all companies like is attention. A common concern is that the company could spend a lot of money on branded content but still not get the attention. Just like Hollywood movies, there's no formula to *guarantee* success. Thankfully, some companies with a large mailing list don't have any content.

If there are two complimentary brands that sell to the same segment of customers, it might be possible to create a project that gets Company A to pay for the project because Company B has the reach. Sell to Company B first and ask for no money, just a promise that they'll promote your project to their consumer base. Now you can approach Company A and say "I can guarantee you x million consumers will experience this project" how much is that worth to you?

8.3.3   THE ADVERTISING-FUNDED FEATURE FILM

Figure 142 shows the movie poster for Circumference[123] a film developed by Tim Clague[124] with the intention of being completely advertising funded. Tim was quite ahead of his time by a number of years and I recently emailed him to ask what lessons he learned. Here's his answers:

> We had contacts in a few large multi-nationals and obviously started by approaching them. The main issue there was internal politics. Some people would like the idea but others would veto it and basically you couldn't get everyone on the same page at the same time. We were trying to raise £360k at that time - 6 advertisers buying a slot for 60k each. This was a good deal compared with ITV and other ad media at the time. It now isn't as ITV has slashed its rates.
>
> Sometimes companies would say that it seemed too cheap, other times that it was too expensive. It became clear though that without an inside contact there was no way to get into large companies. So we teamed up with social media type ad guys - people who normally sell ad packages for websites etc. That was helpful and I think we had a chance there. Luck was against us with the recession and instant drop off of ad spend.

---

[123] http://circumferencemovie.com/
[124] http://projectorfilms.blogspot.com/

The concerns all the way through this process were the same however - a lack of history / a lack of a case study. There wasn't really a way around this.

In the current climate I think you would have to shoot it first and try to sell slots later. But even then I'm not sure it would work - a few new different business strategies have come and gone since and times have changed. I think now you would need a successful online series first (eg Mr Vista[125] style) that you then were going to expand.

Epilogue: We have had to ditch this idea of fundraising altogether and are now trying to raise money using the 'old fashioned' methods. I still think, overall, it could work but you would need these ingredients:

1 - already know marketing people high up in big companies and be trusted by them - i.e. be from a marketing / ad producing background

2 - wait until ad rates have risen more

3 - have had a big online success in some form

4 - still be able to shoot cheaply

5 - have a proven niche audience and approach companies who already reach out to that niche.

Figure 142 Circumference: An advertising-funded movie

_____

[125] http://mrvista.blogspot.com/

8.3.4 TRANSMEDIA IMPLICATIONS AND IMPLEMENTATION

Turning now to your transmedia project, if you plan to create a comic book or flyer as a give-away or hold an event at a local comic book store to promote your project, you might turn to local companies to:

- provide refreshments for the event (local beer, soft drink and fast food companies)

- pay for the printing (local bookshops, local game stores, local printers)

- provide free publicity (newsletters distributed locally by cinemas, supermarkets and book stores, local newspapers)

Remember that you've created valuable content that audiences want to read or events they want to attend. For some companies, being associated with valuable content and the local publicity produced is desirable.

8.3.5 BRANDED ENTERTAINMENT

Branded entertainment is not product placement or support in-kind. It's about having your content - the characters, the storyline and the production values – embody the brand values.

In fact, product placement – having the product or brand logo frequently appear in shot or appear in a contrived way - can be counterproductive because with this entertainment, reducing the brand presence to a "pack shot" or a blatant promotional message costs the content authenticity and credibility – which of course loses the audience.

In March 2010 I attended the SXSW panel "Web Series 2.0" which included Milo Ventimiglia, Melissa Fallon, Wilson Cleveland, Chris Hanada and journalist Andrew Hampp. Among their credits include the web shows Heroes (Sprint), Rock Band 2 (Cisco), It's a Mall World (American Eagle Outfitters), Gossip Girl: Real NYC Stories Revealed (Dove), The Temp Life (Staples), Easy to Assemble (IKEA).

Much of this section contains a distillation of the wisdom from this panel.

8.3.6 PROMOTING AND DISTRIBUTING A BRANDED WEB SERIES

Distribution is a key consideration for a brand looking at a web series: who will watch it, how many people will watch it and where will they watch it? Producers and brands have to manage the desire for their content to "go viral" with the need to convey the correct brand message.

The goal of the web series depends on the brand and this affects the distribution strategy. For example, to achieve maximum exposure it's best to go where the audiences are and this means syndicating the content as much as possible and making it spreadable. Some brands, however, wanted a series to drive traffic to their own micro-site but this only makes sense if it's an e-commerce site where traffic could be converted to sales.

From my personal perspective, using a series to drive direct sales rather than awareness or promoting a brand message immediately damages the content to the point where it very quickly starts to look like advertising which is hence likely to diminish the desired results.

Audience building should start with those most receptive to your content. Hence with branded content, it's important to get the series in front of the brand enthusiasts. In the case of the series *Easy to Assemble*, the producers approached the top ten IKEA fan blogs. Not only were the blog owners likely to be enthusiastic about the show but they were also gateways to thousands of other fans – hence addressing the distribution problem.

To assist further with distribution, the blog owners were told that whichever blog received the most views would be written into the season finale. This obviously incentivized the blogs to promote the series and drove the total views from all the blogs to 3 million views. The video player given to the blogs to embed on their sites was not spreadable and hence it was easy to track views per site.

Using an actor's likeness and personality to promote a web series certainly helps with distribution but many actors or agents were uncomfortable with branded content if it seems like brand endorsement. This is particularly troublesome when negotiated salaries because brand endorsement attracts a much higher salary than a regular acting fee for appearing in a web series. Hence it's important to stress that the actor is not becoming a spokesperson for the brand, he or she is just helping to promote the shows.

Another consideration when contacting actors, is if the web series is promoted on TV because this again can cause some friction around salary terms.

8.3.7   OPPORTUNITIES FOR THE INDIE CREATIVE

For the indie creative, working with the biggest brands is going to be tough because of the trouble in reaching out to them in the first place and then being able to deliver on their needs. It's important when pitching to brands that producers have a complete media strategy of which a web series might be one component. Brands want to know how the audience can be retained between webisodes and between web series.

Consequently, rather than approach brands directly, indies might have better luck in approaching smaller advertising agencies and public relations companies who will have a better understanding of their clients' needs and be able to put your content ideas into a wider perspective. Agencies with business-to-business (B2B) clients or clients in unattractive/commodity industries might be most receptive to branded entertainment because of the difficulty in making these companies interesting or remarkable.

Also consider products with niche or difficult to reach audiences. Traditional advertising channels might be prohibitively expensive. For example, *ThreadBanger* is a web show aimed at people who like sewing, knitting and making their own clothes. In 2010/2011 the show had around 500,000 views per month and was perfect for the Japanese sewing machine manufacture Janome. So successful was show sponsorship that Janome now has a sewing machine with ThreadBanger branding! In 2015, ThreadBanger gets around +1 million views per episode.

A web show is of course different to a web series – the series is usually fictional and "evergreen" in that it provided entertainment however much time passes since its initial release date. Web shows conversely tend to be more topical, current and factual without a narrative arc. Nevertheless, it does illustrate the opportunity for original content to address an under-served audience.

8.4 Crowdfunding

Back in 2010 when I wrote the first edition of this book I had to explain what crowdfunding was. Now I'm quite sure that it's part of the everyday conversation for many readers! Certainly a whole industry has grown up around crowdfunding from consultants to fulfillment companies. A great resource if you're planning a crowdfunding campaign is this one http://www.minivation.co/

Crowdfunding success stories are now becoming commonplace – the most recent at the time of writing being Exploding Kittens[126] which raised almost $9million for the card game. The StoryForward podcast[127] has a great interview with Exploding Kitten's creators Elan Lee and Shane Small which is well worth listening to.

Crowdfunding[128] is a form of sponsored financing because you're asking people to give you money to fund your project... which you may then choose to give away for free.

If you have a million dollar feature film you'd like to make and you're an indie creator, I'm skeptical that you can fully finance it with crowdfunding – even though it has happened. However, taking the transmedia business model approach, you could successfully use crowdfunding to raise, say, around $20k - $250,000 to fund part of your project. The right approach though is to consider when, how much and for what to use you'll use other people's money. Asking too soon or for too little will be just as detrimental as asking for too much.

Most importantly put the audience at the center of the project. **Make your crowdfunding about delivering something for the crowd: you're helping the crowd achieve its ambitions, not it helping you achieve yours**.

Successfully raising money through crowdfunding is all in the planning and your social network. Successful campaigns are those that have already "primed the pump" with supporters ready to be the first in on day 1.   This section presents ideas and information I gained from my work helping people with projects on Kickstarter, conversations with successful Kickstarter creators and from discussions with Andy Baio (Kickstarter's CTO) and Robin Sloan[129]'s panel session at SXSW 2010[130].

---

[126] https://www.kickstarter.com/projects/elanlee/exploding-kittens
[127] http://www.storyforwardpodcast.com/2015/03/12/068-exploding-kittens-scenes/
[128] http://en.wikipedia.org/wiki/Crowd_funding
[129] http://robinsloan.com/
[130] http://www.kickstarter.com/projects/robinsloan/robin-writes-a-book-and-you-get-a-copy

A good article you might also check out are these "*10 Tips for Successful Twitter Fundraising*" by Melissa Jun Rowley[131] at Mashable:

1. Cultivate a Strong Community First
2. State Your Purpose and Your Request Clearly
3. Create Buzz and Excitement
4. Have a Strong Set Up Behind the Scenes
5. Have a Powerful Offline Component
6. Plan, Prepare, Execute, then Get Out of the Way
7. Recognize Volunteers and Donors
8. Keep Contributors Up-to-Date on Progress and Needs
9. Keep Track of Developing Relationships
10. Look for Ways to Improve for Next Time

8.4.1 GETTING STARTED

I'm going to assume that you can't keep asking people for money: plan to only have to do it once. That means that you need to think about what you absolutely, can't work around, specifically and realistically need money for – and then ask once and never again. At least not on this project.

Break down your project into self-contained building blocks. Each block needs a start and end date.

Create a masterplan for your project that takes you from the first published content to the finale. Now look at what you can deliver yourself, what you can deliver with collaboration and what you really need financing for. Now you're ready to follow these four stages:

1. Development (pre-campaign)
2. Production (the campaign period)
3. Post-production (after you have the money)
4. Exhibition

8.4.2 DEVELOPMENT (PLANNING)

Make sure what you plan to make is well defined. It must have a start and end date; it must deliver specific desirable content or an experience.

Plan the Production period and determine the best time to launch your crowdfunding campaign. Make sure that you have the resources required to execute the crowdfunding properly: the people, the places, the time, the content. Don't rush out your request for money and then disappear on vacation expecting that the money will be in on your return!

---

[131] http://mashable.com/2010/02/26/twitter-fundraising/

Make sure that someone on the team has a strong following or a good reputation among the desired community. Don't wait to start your fundraising before connecting to audiences because you're creating too big a mountain to climb. Try to position the crowdfunded content block after you've been able to give something away for free - a demo is very common. Use your own resources first before asking others to give you theirs.

Set your reward levels. Take a look at comparable projects on sites like Kickstarter and see how many people are pledging money and at what price-points. At the time of writing, $25 and $50 often look to be the most popular but of course be sure to have some at the $100, $500, $1000 points too - if appropriate.

Write your pitch and make your plea video. Make it personal, passionate, affecting and informative. Most importantly, if you can, make it about *them*. Make this project about doing something for the crowd. Tell the story around your story. How will this money change your life or the life of others? How will the money help you realize your ambitions (which should be about helping others) and why should anyone care about that? What will your content mean to audiences or others?

Get your social media ready. My recommendation is usually that you Tweet progress using your personal Twitter ID rather than create a new one specifically for the project. This way you make a personal connection to people and you can take followers from project to project.

Update your Twitter background to highlight the fundraising campaign, update your Facebook profile photo, update the project Facebook page etc so that all your online presence have calls-to-action directed at your Kickstarter page.

Write press releases for the start and end of the campaign. Now in 2015 I would never recommend paying for a press release. Social media has completely overtaken the old paid press release but writing one is still a very useful exercise. Great journalists still want to be the first to learn of great stories. But that means you need a good story and it needs to be newsworthy. Being "newsworthy" means you need to tick some or all of the following boxes:

- Relevant – know your journalist! What are they interested in? You can see their articles and read their tweets. Is your project something that will interest them?

- Timing – is it happening now or soon?

- Locality – is this appropriate to the readership? If it's a local newspaper then is something happening in town? If it's a site with global readership, is this something of in the right genre and theme?

- Scale & impact – is what you're doing going to affect a lot of people? What's the impact of doing and not doing your project? How important is this campaign?

- Novelty & human interest – if all else fails, will this news make people laugh or cry? Does it have watercoolability?

Make the journalists' job easy and write the article for her. They can always throw yours away and write their own but reduce as much friction as possible – and have *awesome* photos and graphics available too. Great images are very very important.

8.4.3   PRODUCTION (CAMPAIGN PERIOD)

Design your campaign as you would a story. Plan the campaign period with a beginning, middle and an end. Campaigns typically have lots of activity at the beginning when the call first goes out to find patrons and then at the end when panic sets in! Don't be surprised to find that 50% of your revenue comes in the last 20% of the campaign. Kickstarter knew that having the campaign deadline is a big motivator for getting patrons to commit.

Act 1: Launch the Campaign with a fanfare! Make it exciting and intriguing – make it remarkable so that people want to tell others what you're doing. Consider an offline component that'll generate buzz too – like a launch party. You don't have to hire a private function suite – just find a bar, invite friends and others and bring a soapbox! Wear a T-shirt with a unique Twitter hashtag and encourage everyone to tweet during the evening – create a tweetstorm! And make sure your Kickstarter page is up and running so you can capitalize on the early enthusiasm.

Be quick to respond to questions, comments and patrons.

Act 2: Keep the Dream Alive.

Writing the second act of a script is always the hardest and so it is with the middle of a campaign. You've just hit up everyone you know and you know you'll have to hit them up again at the end. So how do you keep everyone motivated and connected during the middle?

Here's four suggestions:

- Keep the dream alive.
- Give people a reason to retweet.
- Give a mid-campaign sweetner/teaser.
- Combine all of the above.

Keep the Dream Alive.

People want to be on a winning team so frequently update your Kickstarter page with lots of positive energy and upbeat progress reports. We all have those days of anxious self-doubt but don't convey that to the group. You don't have to conceal any problems or disappointments – be open about progress - but greet each hurdle as a challenge rather than an opportunity to moan!

As the donations come in, email each donor to say thank you, ask them if they have any questions and ask for their advice – how can you improve what you're doing? Who else might you ask? Where else might you look for support? People like being asked for their opinion and they like being listen to. Show this love and you'll find that some will take their support to a new level and campaign on your behalf.

For those that donate money above your median price level, ask for their address and send them a handwritten "Thank You" card and maybe a small gift. This isn't something you promised to send, it's a surprise reward for their support.

Look for newsworthy milestones that communicate success. It's sad to say but people usually follow the flock. Few people will read all the details and check out your credentials – they'll back you because they'll trust that someone else in the crowd has done the due diligence. And many will want to see what all the fuss is about. Invent your own success "x amount raised in x days/hours/minutes" – make is sound incredible.

Give people a reason to retweet

Make your tweets about the mission. The mission is the reason why everyone is backing the project. It's the premise of your crowdfunding story: "Animals should not be eaten! Help stop the slaughter http://kickstarterpage #appropriatehashtagforcommunitythatagrees"

Use infographics so your tweets standout in the feed. Make the graphics about the mission.

Your mid-campaign sweetner/teaser.

Deliver a mid-campaign sweetner. Tweet links to content/experiences/opportunities that people want to share.

Do something that has value to the audience you're courting. Again it might be an offline meetup or it could be an online live webcast via Google Hangouts. Give something back and it'll generate buzz, a reason to tweet and cash will come in. Above all – make it valuable and make it interactive.

Act 3: Resolution – the final push. In the closing week, days and hours of your campaign period most people are going to forgive you for making a direct plea for support. In the early stages of the campaign you've been considerate of everyone's time and attention. Now the gloves are off – you have to get that final dollar or you'll lose everything.

Remind everyone how fantastic it's going to be to get the final money and realize *their* ambition –and keep selling that dream because it's infectious. Think positive but remain focused.

8.4.4 POST-PRODUCTION (AFTER YOU'VE RAISED YOUR MONEY)

Migrate your patrons from Kickstarter and onto your community – either Facebook or a forum you've created. Kickstarter is great for fundraising but once the money is in you need to wrap your project around your community and Kickstarter isn't the best place to do that.

A word of caution about Facebook: you'll probably want a Group instead of a Page (it's more egalitarian) and don't forget to continue collecting email addresses. Activating supporters through Facebook with a Facebook post is very ineffective and Facebook continues to review its algorithms for how and what content gets shared.

Allow yourself to be able to contact your community without asking for Facebook's permission.

Although this is the "post production" phase as far as the fundraising, it's during this period that you'll spend the money creating the content you promised. Keep everyone in the loop and keep them engaged: ask questions, ask for suggestions, show what you've done, report how the money is being spent. Be open and honest.

Your patrons have bet on you and they want reassurance they did the right thing: give it to them - reassure them. Remember too that they're in this for the experience; they're living vicariously though you and receiving enormous pleasure in seeing you succeed. Don't deny them that.

One thing that I have found is that just because someone donates money it does not mean they want to help co-create or get involved in discussions. In several cases I've worked on, only about 10% of the people who donated money continued to be actively engaged with the production.

8.4.5   EXHIBITION

The big day is finally here! You have something to show that was paid for by many gracious people. Remember why they contributed and allow your patrons to bask in the reflected glory of your success. Your patrons are part of your team and this is another chance for them to feel good about themselves.

9   APPENDIX 1 – WHERE NEXT FOR REALITY?

"Nothing is real"
John Lennon

9.1   AN AGE OF FLUID REALITY

Stories are the way we make sense of the world. Our minds can't deal with randomness and we see connections, causes and reasons even where there are none. Whether we are happy or sad, positive or negative, this is often the result of the story we construct – it's the meaning we attribute to events and things that without human interpretation have no meaning. So powerful is story that the life we lead today is a result of the stories we told ourselves in the past.

We are entering an age of fluid reality.

Today, our mind can be invited to switch between many parallel realities and anyone can choose to live in whichever reality they feel best suited to. This has always been true to a certain extent but now the imagination is not having to work as hard as it once did – and this allows many more people much greater scope to not only "fantasize" but actually feel like they are living the life they always wanted to live.

As digital representations of the real world become abundant and our view of the "real world" becomes ever more mediated through technology, so our faith in the accuracy of the digital world seems to become greater than our faith in things it claims to represent. This is as troubling as it is enabling. The blending of the real world and virtual representations of it present opportunities to rewrite belief systems and exert influence on an unprecedented scale. We must be sure to use this new power wisely and educate people in its use and misuse.

In the Ukraine, Russia is waging "hybrid warfare" – a mix of traditional rockets and guns camouflaged with denials and grassroots political activism. Propaganda and miss-information have always been vital weapons of war and suppression but today there's an over trust of digital information such that social media will cause us to doubt what we see with our own eyes. Russia says one thing and does another – leaving paralysed traditional players who expect the digital reality to match the physical reality.

The young people who leave liberal, free-thinking democratic societies for the brutally repressive world of ISIS see a different reality from the rest of us. ISIS propaganda has made bigotry and violence exciting to some and exposed European Governments as pathetically out of touch with modern life - as they've always been actually but the fluid, dynamic nature of digital communications exposes their weakness even more. This is a battle of realities is not a battle of "reality on the ground" but a battle of "realities of the mind".

Reality lives in the mind; it lives in the imagination.

9.2 WHAT'S SHAPING REALITY?

The digitization and virtualization of the physical world is reshaping our perception of reality. This takes several forms:

- digital mapping and digitally created environments as exemplified by Virtual Reality (VR)
- digitally created objects and characters overlaid on the real world as exemplified by Augmented Reality (AR)
- virtualization of physical things to create process-oriented models of how the real world works facilitated by the Internet of Things (IoT)
- virtualization of people, groups and communities in the form of social media, avatars and online personas.

Virtual Reality (VR) and Augmented Reality (AR) are well known but less widely known are opportunities afforded by virtualization: Alternative Reality (ALR) and Mixed Reality (MR).

Virtual Reality in the form we commonly understand it as an isolating experience that requires a headset with stereoscopic vision (Oculus, GearVR, Google Cardboard) – we block out the real world and replace it with a live action movie or computer-generated environment.

VR is this generation's ViewMaster. It's a clever trick and part of the wonder and thrill of wearing the headset is our marvel at how easily our mind can be fooled through our eyes. Looking around and up and down and seeing a virtual world around us is fascinating but for now that's usually as much agency as the wearer is afforded. Choices and movement through the virtual world in VR is tricky and uncommon at the moment but in time it will be solved and be more common.

VR headsets and 360 degree movies are generating lots of excitement and it's leading to new discussions about audience agency. Now that the audience (albeit an audience of one in these typically solo player experiences) can look around the virtual space, how do filmmakers tell their story? Now that the frame can't be controlled as precisely as it can with movies & TV, what's the new language of VR cinema?

We have had interactive movies for several decades and they never really took off because usually they're too much work – too disrupted for a satisfying laid-back experience and not enough interaction for a gaming experience. The best examples are those designed with a gaming mindset rather than a filmmaking mindset.

Quite how VR will translate into feature length experiences and multiplayer/multiviewer experiences is yet to play out but this new found alternative reality may open the eyes of some to the possibility that virtual worlds can be all around us too – and not confined to those moments when we wear a headset but alive in real physical spaces.

Augmented reality like VR is again a trick played with our vision. Here though, we view the real world and see images and video overlaid upon it (HoloLens, Meta One, Google Glass). AR is a broader umbrella than VR and doesn't always require us to wear a headset or use our mobile but it does always require a camera to see the world and a screen to display the augmented world (camera's view + image or video overlay).

AR is much less isolating and more social than VR but tends to have many of the limitations of choice and movement.

A less well known enhancement to reality is what could be known as **Alternative Reality (ALR)** - a popular if scary example of which can be seen in the movie, *The Game* (1997), in which Michael Douglas becomes the audience and player in a personalized experience for only him that blends his real life with a fantasy.

ALR heralds from the Alternate Reality Game (ARG) - a format popularized around the turn of this century with games like *The Beast* (for the movie AI) and the off-screen story woven around *The Blair Witch Project*. Here the defining characteristics of the ARG might be considered to be collaborative problem-solving, the wide-ranging agency afforded players and the use of real world artefacts (physical and digital).

ALR doesn't trick the eyes: it works with the imagination. It uses our mind's curiosity and its need to connect the dots. ALR is about human experience design in the broadest possible sense because the goal is to allow an active belief in a parallel world that's interwoven with our everyday world. Nobody is fooled; rather they're given permission to believe.

Imagine the personal and societal benefits of ALR: It has the potential to rewrite the stories we tell ourselves using the right cues at the right time to stimulate positive interpretations of the world. When a lightbulb blows and the depressive thinks "why is everything in my life going wrong?, a digital intervention could flash to the wristwatch "let's have a candle-lit dinner? :)" or a phone call "Trisha let's see the gas lamps on Westminster Bridge! 1807 is going to be a great year for us! I'm certain that we'll soon all have gas light in our homes at the pull of a lever!"

Mixed Reality (MR) is a combination of all the above. Experiences can start in the real world, dip into a completely virtual world, go to an augmented reality and then finish with alternative reality before, hopefully, passing the participant back into their preferred reality.

The project "Meet Lucy" conceived and developed by Nina Simoes and written by David Varela is an example of MR. Here, which participants meet Lucy and her family online, communicating via email, sms and blog posts (ALR) and then can virtually step into Lucy world's (VR) via the Oculus headset and Unity (the software that generates the virtual world). Coordinating all this is Conducttr which even personalizes the VR experience by telling the Unity engine who and what to render based on the participants online interactions.

9.3 WHAT OPPORTUNITIES DO ALTERNATIVE & MIXED REALITY OFFER?

Alternative Reality and Mixed Reality offer an opportunity to create **experiences that are connected, personalized, participatory and social**. Importantly the experiences fit around the audience and their habits and interests, not the other way around.

Although the possibility to operate commercial services that use AR and MR is revolutionary (and at this time only possible with Conducttr), the audience and consumer behaviours that underpin the opportunities are age old.

Using transmedia storytelling, new opportunities arise for connected, personalized, participatory and social experiences can that reinvent traditional industries like:

- Entertainment
- Advertising
- Education
- Healthcare

9.4 REINVENTING ENTERTAINMENT

The problem with the entertainment industry is that it's still broadcasting and not listening.

The phenomenal rise in the popularity of gaming (including Twitch streaming and live gaming); the outpouring of "user-generated content"; the rise of the six-figure-income "YouTuber"; the rise in popularity of escape room experiences;   and the popularity of communities like TripAdvisor and Reddit... they all point to a new empowered, self-actualized audience that is mostly ignored, placated or sidestepped by broadcasters.

TV audiences are getting older and younger generations are not watching TV – this is a fact across all continents. This is correspondingly causing problems for advertisers who want to reach that younger generation but can't do so as well as they once could on TV.

The opportunity for TV is to become the "cut scenes" inside a persistent experiential worlds. Instead of reluctantly adding a website to support a TV show, broadcasters should create massively participatory interactive experiences that add TV content. Just as mobile is now the "first screen", so transmedia experiences will become the norm. Why? Because this firmly places the audience at the centre of the experience and allows greater scope for a spectrum of revenue opportunities – of which advertising may or may not be the primary source of financing.

9.5 REINVENTING ADVERTISING

The problem with today's advertising technology is that it focuses on the needs of the advertiser, not the consumer.

For all the claimed innovation, most adtech is really just about shouting louder or taking the consumer's watch and telling them the time. In fact the worst offenders are those technologies that suck user-generated content from the community, aggregate it and regurgitate it for the needs of the brand. It's like arriving at a party and giving the host flowers stolen from their garden.

Similarly, tracking consumers across platforms by using cookies belongs in the 1990's.

Hopefully nobody stalks their friends across the internet nor in real life and yet we know what to buy them as a birthday gift. This is because we have a relationship. Today's advertising technology doesn't seek a relationship, it seeks data and hopes that by analyzing enough data an insight into someone's preferences will be gained. Yet we know that many consumers have multiple online identities and the technology can be defeated or fooled. As education and society shift towards greater media and technology literacy and mistrust of surveillance, tracking with cookies is going to be consigned to the past where it belongs.

What alternative reality and mixed reality experiences offer is the opportunity to form real relationships. These are formed by giving back to the community and insights are formed through willing consumer participation.

Consumer participation in this context means creating brand-sponsored, empowering experiences that invite people to connect with each other and connect to the issues that matter to them. Some brands do this from time-to-time in the form of live events and such like but they tend to be campaign-based which means customers are allowed to get excited for a short period and then they get abandoned. Still, better to have periods of giving than never at all.

See this short demonstration, Connected Brand Experiences, for an example of how things might be done differently.

9.6   REINVENTING EDUCATION

The problem with today's education is that it was designed centuries ago for people who would go to work in a factory.

As manufacturing industries declined and service industries increased, the lesson topics changed but the process of education didn't. So now we have schools that feel like prisons. Mobile phones, social media, games and responsive systems of all kinds are all around us in homes, workplaces, shopping malls... but not in schools where phones must be switched off and everyone must sit in silence and listen to teacher. So the students have one of the most powerful computers of all time in their pocket but they're not shown how to use it wisely.

Today's students are growing up in a world that is changing faster than at any time in the past and the jobs they'll do when they leave may not have been invented yet. Many students known this and the uncertainty leads to insecurity and in the worse cases hopelessness and depression and suicide. We have a duty of care to make students more mentally resilient to uncertainty and give them skills they can take to any job: critical thinking, collaborative problem solving, negotiation skills, conflict resolution, mindfulness and so on.

Using mixed reality-based education we can blend formal and informal learning spaces to create an environment of engaging continuous learning. By putting the student at the center and using transmedia storytelling we create dynamic, team-based, collaborative problem solving, participatory environments that encourage exploration, examination, reasoning, debate and negotiation – vital skills in the modern workplace and that of the future. The teacher too is liberated - no longer expected to be the font of all knowledge who can never be wrong but a mediator who guides and encourages student exploration so that they find solutions for themselves.

9.7   REINVENTING HEALTHCARE

The problem with the current trend in digital healthcare is that it's fixated on patient data and encouraging people to exercise.

Just like the pharmaceutical industry, everyone's looking for a quick win in the shape of an easy pill to swallow: the premise is that more information will lead to better decisions. And maybe it does in some cases but it's not the only answer. More information doesn't address motivation or mood. And leader boards might motivate the competitive but coming last can reinforce low-self-esteem in others.

The stories we tell ourselves affect our mental state and our mind affects our emotional and physical wellbeing. Illnesses like addiction, depression, and obesity are best addressed through mindfulness techniques that rewire our perception of reality to write a new story and replace the corrosive stories.

More data won't fix a broken heart or a miss-wired brain. Pervasive, mixed reality stories can. Immersive real world experiences that use real-time and behavioral data and simulation techniques - can send positive reinforcement, encouragement and inspire compassion, love and gratitude. The future of healthcare lies in a partnership between the storyteller and the patient in which imagination drives enthusiasm, understanding and better habits.

9.8   CONCLUSION

The ideas presented in this document are intended to inspire and encourage new avenues of inquiry in traditional industries that can be radically improved through the use of alternative and mix reality.

Our unique pervasive entertainment platform, Conducttr, offers a storytelling and gaming layer for the real world which, combined with real-time participatory transmedia storytelling, can enrich lives.

10 APPENDIX 2 – TRANSMEDIA FOR CHANGE

10.1 TRANSMEDIA FOR CHANGE

Transmedia for Change (T4C) is an umbrella term that encompasses transmedia activism (change in society or community) and personal growth (change in lifestyle, personal development). Underlying T4C is the belief that stories matter, that those stories need to be told to the right people at the right time and most importantly that projects should offer a pathway to success.

As I stated in my early post, *Where Next for Reality*, nothing is real: the reality we experience is grounded in the stories we tell ourselves. So T4C advocates for storytellers to a. engage audiences with positive messages that inspire and motivate better choices and b. provide solutions.

Creating impact ought to be the factual storyteller's overriding goal. It's too easy to say a project's goal is to "create awareness" without articulating what change that awareness should bring about nor how the aware should take action. Take for example projects that say they want to raise awareness about privacy. How many provide a real debate about the trade-offs between privacy and security or privacy and convenience or privacy and price? And many of these privacy projects on the one hand attack Facebook while on the other use the player's Facebook information there to create the wow effect of the experience to supposedly "highlight the dangers". Isn't that contradictory? Like explaining to someone the danger of gunpowder while getting them to light a firework. Where's the wow in these privacy projects without the privacy invasion? My point here is only that the makers should go beyond awareness as a goal and think how their projects can deliver solutions. Telling forgotten people's stories or allowing people to tell their stories isn't enough – it's still just telling and not doing.

We should use our stories to engage and our technology to empower. Rather than imagine the interactive documentary (idoc) project as a beacon, it ought to be a solution.

10.2 NO WEBSITE SHOULD BE AN ISLAND

A problem I see with many webdocs is that they are beautiful works of art to be admired but likely have little impact. Although they're online and clickable many feel like gallery pieces that showcase the integration of art and technology – amazing data visualizations and smooth flowing, storytelling user interfaces but they kind of just leave me admiring the craft while disengaged with the issue. I never feel like I really enter the story because the prowess of the design draws attention to itself and away from the message.

So what if someone spends a prolonged amount of time on a website if really what you want them to do is go into the streets? How can they take the message with them? And importantly how can they take that message to others?

If future projects are to create greater impact, they need to connect to people where the people are – they're mobile, they're in the real world and of course they're across platforms.

10.3 IN RUDE HEALTH

In our project for the Mexican health authority, we're connecting a mobile and desktop game to patient visits to HIV clinics. There is no typical hub website, it's the patient at the center of the experience (i.e. their life!) and orbiting them are the platforms they use. When players visit a clinic, they have a "VIP pass" on their phone (a reward and incentive for taking part) that enables them to jump the line and doctors send an SMS to receive a single-use 5-character code that is given to the player to "check-in" at the clinic (which must be completed within 10 mins before the code is deactivated).

Far from being an "awareness campaign", this is a project intended to change the behavior of men – encouraging them to negotiate better with sexual partners and track their attitudes and behaviors against three sets of game mechanics so that we can see which mechanics are the most effective in increasing the frequency of clinic visits.

Note that everything plays out anonymously – safeguarding the privacy of participants – while still providing a referral mechanism for players to invite friends and allow us to track the biggest referrers and which mechanic inspires the most referrals.

All this is created with Conducttr from off-the-shelf functions – massively reducing the cost of deployment and instantly being massively scalable and secure.

Join us to discuss these ideas or present your own at this year's Conducttr Conference on October 16th 2015 in London, UK.

11 APPENDIX 3 – INVISIBLE MARKETING

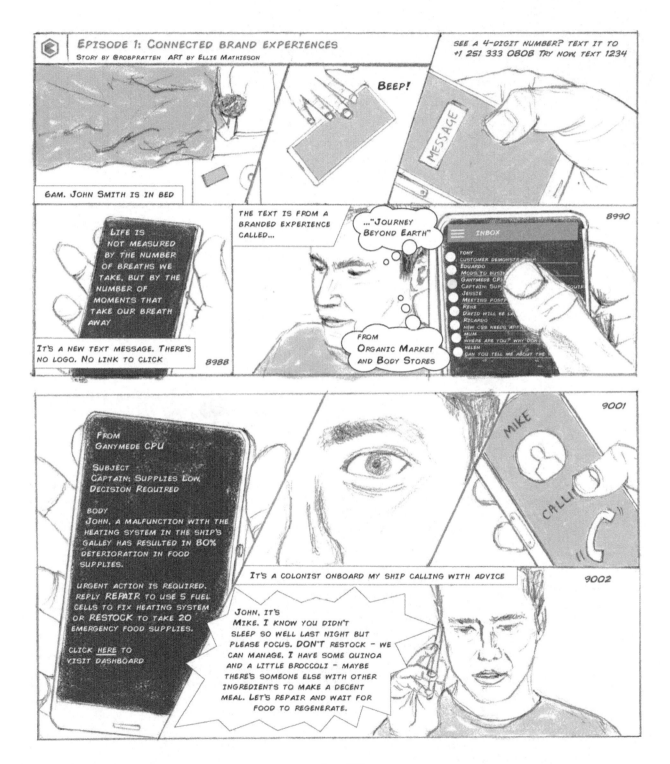

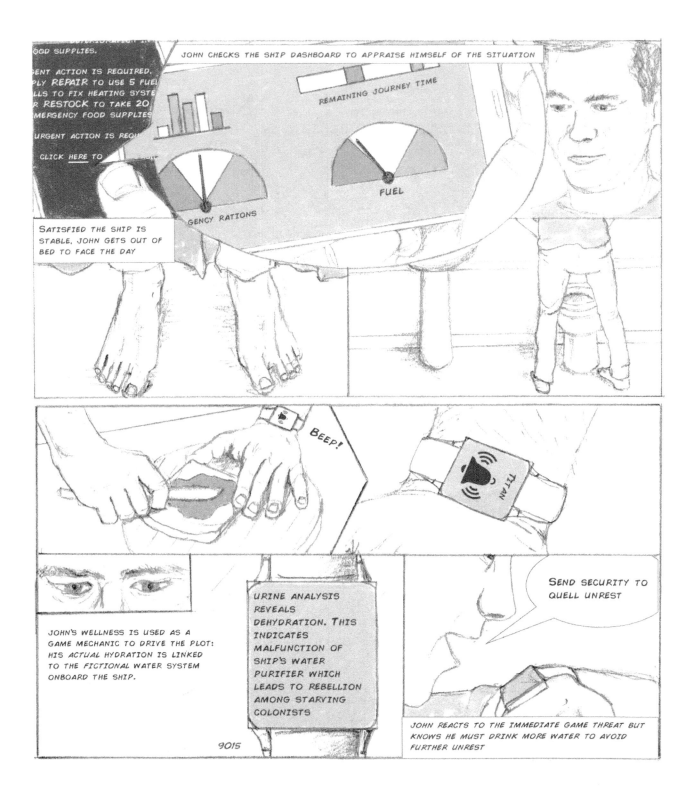

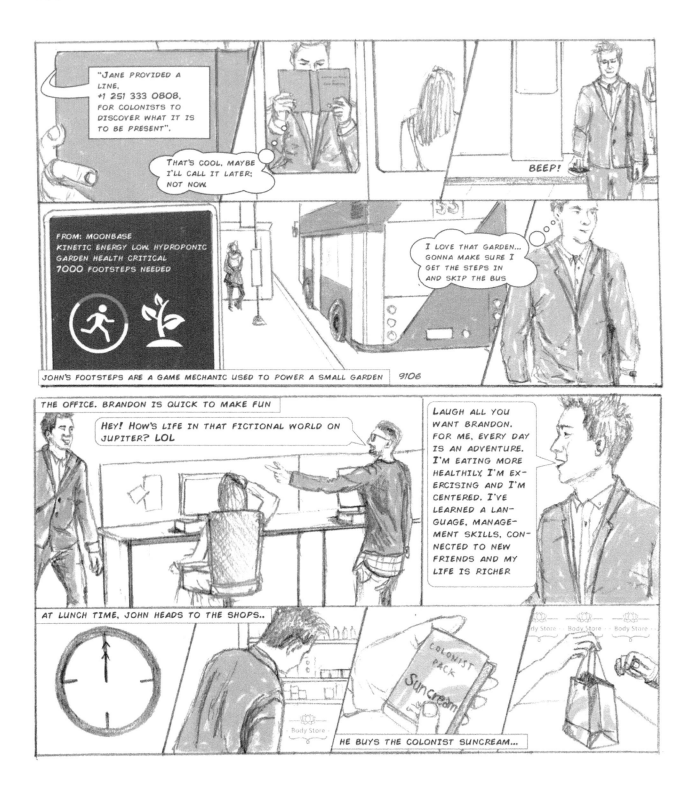

12 ABOUT THE AUTHOR

Robert Pratten is founder and CEO of Transmedia Storyteller Ltd – creators of Conducttr, the multiplatform interactive storytelling and gaming platform.

Robert's experience uniquely places him at the intersection of entertainment, marketing and technology: he brings more than 25 years' experience as a marketing consultant and expertise in Intelligent Networks having formally advised clients such as Ericsson and Telcordia on international pricing, positioning and market entry strategies.

In 2000, he left Europe's leading telecoms consultancy firm to attend the London Film School and since wrote, produced and directed two award-winning, critically acclaimed feature films - London Voodoo (2004) and Mindflesh (2008).

In 2011 he produced the original transmedia proof-of-concept project for Conducttr, Lowlifes.

Today he is an internationally recognized thought-leader in transmedia storytelling - regularly speaking at conferences including the World Innovation Conference, SXSW Interactive, FIPA, Storyworld and also to transmedia meetup groups to encourage and inspire a new era of independent creative thinking. Companies that he's consulted with in the area of transmedia storytelling include Canal+Spain, Disney, Endermol, Toyota, MindLab, Lifelike and many more.

Please feel free to connect on Twitter @robpratten or via the forum at conducttr.com

CPSIA information can be obtained
at www.ICGtesting.com
Printed in the USA
LVOW03s0505101215

466204LV00005B/74/P